STILL WET
BEHIND
THE EARS

By the same author

Must I Go Down to the Sea Again?

ISBN 0 229 11767 8

Dedicated to reluctant sailors everywhere, this book reveals the hilarious truth about family cruising. Lesley Black's unerring eye for the funny side of sailing could spell the end of serious yachting as we know it.

STILL WET BEHIND THE EARS

Lesley Black

Illustrated by Mike Peyton

ADLARD COLES
8 Grafton Street, London W1

Adlard Coles
William Collins Sons & Co. Ltd
8 Grafton Street, London W1X 3LA

First published 1986 in hardback in Great Britain by
Fernhurst Books, 53 High Street, Steyning, West Sussex
Paperback edition published by Adlard Coles 1990

British Library Cataloguing in Publication Data

Black, Lesley
  Still wet behind the ears.
  Sailing
  I. Title
  797.124

ISBN 0–229–11858–5

Printed and bound in Great Britain by
Hartnolls Limited, Bodmin, Cornwall

Contents

1

Buy, buy blues . . .

I was once taking coffee with a non-sailing friend when she received, by the same post, her gas, electricity and telephone bills. As she gazed morosely at the offending documents and wondered aloud how she was going to keep body and soul together through the coming months, I felt moved to offer some words of fellow feeling for her predicament. She eyed me somewhat coldly. "I don't know what you've got to complain about", she said, with a certain testiness. "You've got one more yacht than I have, for a start . . ." And so I had – and that, of course, was why my own bank statement was lying at home, hidden behind the clock, unopened.

It is not really so surprising that sailing is still regarded by the uninitiated as a rich person's sport. Although it is not long since a boat was sold purely on its fine lines and solid seaworthiness, nowadays when you look through the glossy advertisements there's so much emphasis on luxury fittings and optional extras that we'll soon be getting a jacuzzi as standard on a new craft.

We can't all buy in this class, though, and if we had to there'd be a lot less congestion in the harbours. An extremely affluent pal once offered a nugget of advice to me on this topic. "In my opinion", said this budding Onassis, nodding sagely, "it's sheer self-indulgence to spend more than, say, £30,000 on a boat. . . well, on one's *main* boat anyway". As this was several years back and at the time the sum mentioned would have purchased a pretty lavish family home and probably furnished it too, I saw no reason to argue the point. Even today, inflation notwithstanding, it remains a dictum to which I fully adhere, entirely through lack of option to do otherwise.

Our very first floating investment, swapped for a tent, was a derelict two-seater canoe which had apparently been knocked together by a schoolboy carpenter on an off-day. By the time she'd sunk under us twice and capsized over us three times we'd agreed unanimously that she was not our idea of fun, but we'd also patched her up sufficiently to form part of a crafty trade-in deal on a small sailing dinghy. And so our laborious climb towards the heady ranks of the keelboat brigade had begun.

It was in buying the first of these that real money was at last involved, and it also gave us our first taste of the more orthodox techniques of selling. The husband and wife disposing of this cramped 24-footer formed a perfect team as they led us on our tour of inspection. *He* set to work on the Skipper, extolling the boat's handling qualities and solid construction, and flattering him with liberal use of technical terms and sailing jargon . . . "Of course, I don't need to tell *you* about the stiffness to windward you get with hard chine . . ." *She*, meanwhile, was softening me up below decks, taking me through every galley fitting and locker, stretching me out on bunks that were a foot too short for comfort and assuring me with a gay laugh that I would very soon stop stunning myself on the coachroof at every turn and grow to love the intimate ambience of the saloon. Then, together, they moved in for the kill. "We knew you'd like a sail to get the feel of her," he said, eyes twinkling, "so my wife has made up just a small picnic lunch . . ." "No trouble at all", she interrupted quickly as we went to protest, "It's only a simple *coq au vin* and a bottle or two of Riesling, so *please* don't feel you're under any obligation to us . . ."

It was all part of the game, and we learned the lesson well. A couple of seasons later, when it was our turn to sell, I heard myself handing out the same well-tried lines, including the free meal. It's hard to tell a chap his boat is not up to scratch when the crumbs from his wife's *quiche Lorraine* are still sticking to your chin. We were less generous in the alcoholic department, however, as we soon discovered that too much largesse can lead to the development of a frivolous, loose-tongued atmosphere in which it's all too easy for the seller to carelessly let slip a few of the faults he's studiously omitted from his chat-up routine, or for the prospective buyer to reveal that he could go up another few hundred, if pushed. I've seen my Skipper, cockles thoroughly warmed and glowing with friendship for a fellow sailor, practically forcing money onto a seller who, fortunately feeling equally genial, smilingly waved the offer aside.

Although it is accepted that we may embroider or dissemble just a little during our salestalk, we do draw the line at outright lies. Even amongst the professionals it is extremely rare to find a salesman who'll resort to the 'lovely little driver, the wife's runabout actually' patter of the used-car merchant. We've met it only once, when the boat in question was a catamaran that seemed to us very well priced for its size and potential. The fast-talking broker handed us some convincing and fluent chat, assuring us that the general air of tattiness and the seaweed clinging to the floorboards were entirely due to the present owner being too busy with his new boat to keep up the strict maintenance schedule he normally insisted upon. Luckily for us he was called to the phone while still in full flight and as we strolled around her, already feeling that *frisson* of excitement that comes with the closing of a smart deal, we met one of those flat-capped, weary-eyed old salts that so often pop up in boatyards, paintpot in hand.

"Thinking of buying her, are you?" he enquired, raising a shaggy brow.

"Well, yes . . ." we said, eagerly. "Of course, we realise she's not in perfect condition but . . ."

"Be a b. . . . . miracle if she was," he interrupted with a dismissive sniff. "She was on the bottom a long time before they salvaged her and nobody's been near her since . . ."

It was a useful lesson. It taught us to listen with only half an ear to any extravagant claims, and check them out later with the bloke on the boat next door. Of course he too may have been well-rehearsed, but that doesn't always work – as we have found out to our cost. When our lovely, but elderly, 'Mary Lunn' was on the market recently we warned our pals to stay well clear during inspection sessions and keep their witty remarks to themselves. However, a steady hour of hard selling went for nought when the one chap we hadn't briefed strolled into view and shouted cheerily, "Good heavens, Les, that's the first time I've seen you without a paintbrush in your hand for weeks! Did you ever manage to trace that oil-leak by the way?" Some

A perfect team.

frantic eyebrow semaphoring on my part made him realise his blunder and he sprinted for cover, leaving the Skipper and me to repair the damage with some slightly hysterical laughter. He wasn't finished, though, for just as our guests were promising to "go off and do some serious thinking" he came back and, seeing me emerging from the hatch apparently alone, yelled, "Whoops! Sorry about that! Can I talk freely now, or are they still within earshot?" I must assume their thinking took an even more serious tone after that, for they departed without a smile and no offer was forthcoming.

The final delivery of a new boat should be a time of joy, but often this too is fraught with problems. When we sold our old motor-sailer, the new owners, understandably nervous about bringing an unfamiliar and elderly craft across the Irish Sea in the middle of winter, elected instead to engage a hefty and experienced delivery crew to do the job for them. The weather that greeted this stalwart team's arrival was so appalling that we fully expected the mission to be aborted at once. However, they scoffed at the very idea and assured us that November gales were meat and drink to them – a claim somewhat belied by their decision to spend the first night in the warmth and comfort of the local hotel rather than aboard the boat itself. But, to give them their due, the next morning at the stroke of half past eleven they were breakfasted and ready to go. Things took a turn for the worse when they arrived at the boat.

"I say, old chap", said their leader, backing up the companionway steps in alarm, "Are your carpets usually awash?"

A brief search soon established the cause of the paddling pool effect as a fractured sea-cock. This was readily replaced with a new one, but to no avail. Our fearless crew, their nerve broken, were already hotfooting it to the airport and home, leaving us to break the happy news to our would-be purchasers. They took it with a surprising degree of fortitude and agreed instead to receive the boat by road, at our expense of course, and so another expected profit bit the dust.

Doing your own delivery trip, while ensuring a greater degree of commitment to the project, in no way guarantees success either. When bringing our new boat 'Chancer' home from Scotland this year, we were almost defeated at the outset by the fine logistical planning required to get us and our

"Thinking of buying her, are you?"

mountain of gear to the boat without leaving a car expensively abandoned somewhere on the wrong side of the Irish Sea. We solved that one by bribing a friend to sail us there, which seemed an appropriate and stylish way to make the journey. Sadly, we reckoned without foul weather and the fact that we hadn't set foot in a boat that season and so had not acquired our annual sea-legs, with the result that the entire Black family spent a fair proportion of the trip sitting in a silent line in the cockpit, clutching plastic buckets. We made good time, though, and so arrived at our destination far too soon. 'Chancer' had been undergoing some repairs and a respray, delays had set in, and when we reached her she was still not launched. So the first few days of the bare week we'd allowed for the job were spent living aboard a boat that was still swinging gaily in a travel hoist in a dreary yard littered with rusted trailers and assorted yachting debris. It was a novel experience, but not one which I would wish to repeat. For a start there was the lack of privacy brought about by us working inside the boat while a team of yard-men toiled outside, with all of us trying to be on our best behaviour and not let slip an incautious oath when dropping a spanner on our toes. Secondly, since the ship's heads were clearly out of bounds, we had to make do with the frankly primitive facilities provided for the workmen. Believe me, it's no fun to wake in the middle of a rainy night and know that the only way to achieve personal comfort is to climb down a near-vertical ladder, torch in teeth, and grope your way to a verminous lean-to with a leaking flush. Surprisingly, the kids enjoyed it all, inventing a game called 'nuclear survivors'. They would disappear on lengthy scavenging hunts, returning with pockets weighed down with pinless shackles and threadless bolts which the Skipper would lob into the distance under cover of darkness, only to have them returned, in triumph, the following day. It was an immense relief when at last launching day arrived and, glad to feel the clean sea breeze on our faces, we set off down the Clyde for home.

The weather had other ideas, however. Our refreshing wind soon piped up to a challenging blow and several attempts to get a few miles behind us were aborted as we slunk into the nearest haven to try to sort out the vicious weather helm 'Chancer' was suddenly displaying. We'd had no warning of this from the previous owner and, mystified, we tried out every sail pattern imaginable before we at last discovered the cause. It was me,

ramming the largest fenders into the stern locker with a well-placed boot, thus rendering the rudder stock virtually immobile.

The wind finally veered astern with the promise of a fast run home and we cast off the warps to leave into a chilly grey dawn. 'Chancer' seemed happy enough at first, but the wind increased rapidly and big seas began to roll up astern. As the Skipper usually revels in this roller-coaster sailing while the rest of us endure it in tight-lipped silence, I was surprised to see that he seemed a bit grim-jawed too.

"What's wrong?" I enquired in that sharp tone that sailing wives seem to acquire so easily.

"There's nothing *wrong*," he said. "It's just that I had a bit too much coffee before we left, and I'm not too happy about giving you the helm in these conditions while I . . . er . . . attend to it, that's all."

It was at precisely that moment that we discovered, by means of a truly spectacular broach, that we were carrying too much canvas. Fortunately the children were firmly harnessed and avoided being hurled overboard. I, to my eternal shame, was not clipped on and it was only the vice-like grip of my daughter's petrified fingers that saved me from a watery finale. A second wave which lifted us and flung us along broadside caused our beautiful solid teak table, so much admired during our buying period, to break loose from its mountings and begin crashing back and forth below decks. Eventually, after a heroic struggle on the foredeck, the Skipper managed to drop the jib and, with some sort of order restored, I took the helm. Feeling my confidence gradually returning I gave what I hoped was an encouraging smile all round and said, "Right, we're OK now. I'll steer and you can make that trip to the heads if you like . . ." The Skipper winced visibly.

"Forget it", he muttered, a trifle sheepishly. "It's too late now." I wouldn't be borrowing *his* oilskins for a while anyway.

Grateful at having got off so lightly, we headed for the nearest port only to find, as we at last picked out the seawall through the waves and spray, that there were two black balls hoisted at the storm-tossed entrance.

"What does that mean?" I yelled, as we bucked and plunged and my eye took in the white-topped waves breaking across the tiny gap in the walls and the blessedly calm water beyond. "Can't we go in?"

"Don't worry," he responded, squaring his shoulders resolutely. "They'd have to mine the approaches to stop *me* going in . . ."

Our teenage son lifted his head from his foetal huddle beneath the sprayhood. "*And* hang out a string of tattered corpses," he said, with feeling.

Carefully we lined ourselves up for the run, waited nervously for a brief lull in the swell and then gunned the engine and shot through the gap, missing the port-hand wall by inches. The

It was a humdinger of a party . . .

crowd of sightseers on the pier head raised a cheer for us, to which the Skipper responded with a nonchalant wave. Then he turned to me with a grin. "Here, you berth her," he said, giving me back the tiller. "I think I *will* make that trip to the heads after all."

It was a further two days before we made our final run – one to calm our splintered nerves and one to get rid of the resultant hangover – but at last we sailed into our own yacht club basin, tied up and waited to regale our friends and fellow mariners with tales of our seamanship and endurance. We were not given the chance to get started. Although our friends came to welcome us in droves – at one point it seemed that 'Chancer' might founder at the quayside under the sheer weight of well-wishers – they were more interested in inspecting the fittings and commenting on the colour schemes than in our catalogue of disasters.

I'm told that it developed into a real humdinger of a party, but the Skipper and I missed it all. We subsided into two somnolent heaps in opposite corners of the saloon and our only contributions to the revelry were occasional gobbling snores as we gave ourselves up to the utter exhaustion that comes with final release from mental stress.

One friend did take the trouble to wake us up before leaving. "I just wanted to congratulate you on your new boat," he said. "She's lovely. You must be feeling over the moon."

Well, I'd like to feel we were over the worst, at least.

2

The boat buyer's glossary

Mystified by the classifieds? Want to know what really lies behind the high-flying prose of those tempting small ads? Follow the Black guide to a number of well-worn selling lines, and how to read between them . . .

Design and construction

Familiar phrase	*Probably means*
Excellent compromise cruiser/racer...	Too slow to win, too spartan to enjoy.
Ideal family cruiser.	Offers same heady excitement as driving Morris Minor.
Fine racing record.	Everything over-stressed, or broken.
Built on traditional lines.	Narrow, gloomy, with numerous untraceable leaks.
Sturdy and popular boat.	She's no looker!
Comfortable craft.	Sluggish.
Great appeal for serious wanderer considering live-abroad situation.	Has all the airy grace of a block of council flats.
Rare version of legendary design.	Modified by home handyman, super-structure resembling garden shed.

Ideal first-time purchase.	Basic bath-tub.
Single-handed beach launched and recovered.	Have hernia, must sell.
A real head-turner.	Always at the back of the racing fleet.
For the discerning owner.	Only masochistic oddballs need apply.
A true collector's piece.	Belongs in a museum.

Fittings and equipment

All modern navigational gear.	If the power fails, you're on your own.
Fridge/freezer/all-electric water supply.	Ditto.
Running H&C water, showers etc.	Heavy condensation problems.

Great appeal for serious wanderer.

Sleeps 6-8.

Compact/efficient/well-planned galley.	Meagre work surfaces, minimal stowage, and sited to ensure buttock-to-buttock contact with navigator at chart table.
Convenient navigation area.	See 'galley', reference buttock interlocking.
Cabin heating.	Light all gas rings and open oven door.
Sleeps 6/8.	Has comfortable berths for four, the rest hang from the rafters or kip on a rota basis.
Extensive sail wardrobe, some never used.	Most tattered and threadbare, storm jib still in original bag, with all hanks seized.

Usual inventory.

Usual inventory.	Has barest essentials.
Many extras.	Will throw in dubious dinghy, some well-thumbed charts, and hand-bearing compass with obscuring bubble.
Inventory too comprehensive to list.	Owner can't face thought of clearing out clutter of years.

Home comforts

Cleverly designed interior.	Everything converts into something else, causing complete chaos in process.
Cunningly concealed stowage space.	Locker doors guaranteed to mangle fingers without allowing access to contents.

Generous stowage.	Has numerous deep caverns in which precious items disappear without trace.
Deceptively spacious.	Looks roomy, but isn't.
Light, airy saloon.	No privacy. Start sewing curtains.
All the charm of an old-timer.	None of the basic necessities of modern living.
Amateur interior.	Bungled interior.
Elegant and luxurious accommodation.	Pretentious gin-palace.
Recently completely refurbished.	Paint dribbles everywhere.
All new upholstery.	In colour you'll loathe on sight.
Needs some cosmetics.	Has finish of primitive dug-out.

Present condition

Very clean.	Owner has done heroic deodorising job.
One fastidious owner from new.	Has had difficulty selling.
Maintained regardless expense.	Owner still white-faced from recent yard bill.
Strong as the day she was built.	Remember the Titanic?
Interesting history.	Salvage job.
Most of the hard work done.	The expensive work remains
Ready to win.	Hasn't won yet.
Sound in all major areas.	She floats.
Needs some attention.	Needs major refit.
Needs major refit.	She doesn't float.

Getting down to the nitty-gritty

Save thousands.	Spend tens of thousands.
Very seriously for sale.	The price is no laughing matter.

Price on application.	If you have to ask, you can't afford it.
No offers.	Owner over confident. Let him stew for a while.
Offers over £x.	Owner would accept considerably less than £x.

A true collector's piece.

Try offers.	Owner getting worried.
Sensible offers.	Owner entering pleading stage.
Realistically priced.	Owner reluctantly acknowledging grim truth.
Now much reduced price.	Owner desperate.
Price fully negotiable.	Anything vaguely legal considered.

Berth included.

The reasons why

Owner buying larger.	Owner bragging.
Emigration forces sale.	No comeback if keel drops off in a week.
Redundancy forces sale.	Owner prematurely committed to new boat. This one now superfluous to requirements.
Business forces sale.	Employer, suspicious of frequent sick leave on sunny afternoons during sailing season, forces sale.

Illness forces sale.

Genuine reason for sale.

Very reluctantly for sale.

Partnership split forces sale.

Boat rolls like pig. Seasick family forces sale.

Bank manager forces sale.

Wife forces sale.

Divorce pending.

Oddities and absurdities

A rare opportunity to purchase . . .

All sister ships succumbed to age years ago.

Unique craft.

Weird one-off.

Well-known locally.

Has taken gouges out of every boat in the marina.

Well-mannered boat.

Always lets others lead the way.

Real sea-going boat.

Do not attempt to sail this 35-footer in the village pond.

Must be seen/inspection recommended.

Who but the clinically deranged would buy a boat without seeing it first?

Truly one for the yachting connoisseur.

Blatant flattery. If you fall for this one you're beyond any I can offer!

3

Grounds for complaint

It should never have happened in the first place, of course. But at the end of a sunny weekend's pottering, with Monday morning still a comfortable distance away, it's easy to drift into complacency as one meanders idly back home. We raised our glasses in happy salute as our fellow wanderer veered off to pick up his mooring and we turned our bows towards the pontoons to off-load stores. Ten minutes later, glancing up in relief at having hurled the last over-stuffed stuff-bag ashore, I was surprised to see our friend pretty much where we'd left him, while a rubber dinghy buzzed purposefully in our direction.

"Pete says, could you give him a hand?" its occupants panted, as they bounced up alongside. "He seems to have a bit of a problem. . . "

He had indeed. Arriving at the scene, eager to go into our rescue routine, we learned the cause of it. Being in no hurry, and noticing an unfamiliar and interesting-looking boat lying to one of our visitor's moorings, Pete had decided to take a few minutes to do a critical survey of her lines. What he failed to note was that (a) said mooring had been out of position for some time, and (b) said boat was 'floating' in a strangely erect manner, pointing in a direction not dictated by either wind or tide, and with several inches of her hull revealed. These sad facts he had learned the hard way, fifty yards off. It took a while for our mocking laughter to subside and for the dinghy crew to pay out a long line between us without throttling themselves, but at last both ends were secured and the big heave began. We tugged, they yelled, we ignored them and pulled harder, water boiled and frothed and blue smoke poured out as we piled on more pressure. Hanging from a backstay I bawled a running commentary on our progress, or lack of it, until this was brought to an abrupt halt by the rope snapping with a loud twang, the free end whistling back and knocking the breath out of me. We looked round for the dinghy crew to join us up for another go, but they had apparently more urgent matters to occupy them – like the bar being open – and had buzzed off. It was then that we remembered the club's shallow-draft rescue launch, on a mooring nearby. Cursing himself for not having thought of it before, my Skipper tied us up to her buoy, leaped aboard, tossed the mooring over, and roared away, leaving me behind. I yelled a protest but was too late, as he now had other problems to worry about. The launch was jammed in reverse gear and he made only a hundred yards before the tiller, unable to withstand the strain of doing fifteen knots backwards, snapped off in his hand. He hurled over the anchor just in time to prevent her from going ashore, but now he, like me, was marooned.

His string of expletives was interrupted by the 'phut-phut' of another engine as a new would-be saviour arrived to assist. But he was deep-keeled, had no dinghy, and could do no more than circle sympathetically, lost in thought. His revery was interrupted when his circling became a little too generous and he also found the shallow patch and curtseyed to a halt. Scarcely had that skipper and crew gathered themselves from a heap on the cockpit sole when along came yet another boat. This time we seemed to be in luck for he had both a powerful engine and a fine, sturdy dinghy to offer us. There was just one snag – he was alone and could not man both boat and dinghy at the same time, so, waving aside our shouted warnings, he edged towards the rescue launch to pick up my skipper to help.

With immense skill and precision he manoeuvred gently forward until he was just close enough for my man to make an agile leap for the bowsprit. Very impressed, we all gave a cheer and he responded with a triumphant bow, and paid for his moment's inattention, as his keel settled snugly into the silt.

There was a stunned silence as we assessed the chaos we had created – we now had four craft aground, one disabled and me a helpless onlooker. If this kept up we'd soon be able to *walk* ashore, stepping from boat to boat. Feeling it was now up to me to do something sensible, I decided to return to the pontoons and come back with a powerful motor boat and a heavy crew, even if I had to kill for it. I turned the key of our trusty Volvo. It refused to start.

But our shame was not yet complete. Standing on our respective foredecks and wondering what on earth to do next, we reached the collective decision that the blame for the entire fiasco lay with Pete and his abortive tour of inspection.

"Why did you have to go over there anyway?" we yelled, pointing accusing fingers at the visiting boat. "Couldn't you see that the b– thing was high and dry? Just *look* at it." And we all looked, and it wasn't. It was bobbing happily, bows swinging round into the breeze, and so the uncomfortable truth dawned. The tide had turned, and if anyone had had the wit to consult the tables before embarking on this enthusiastic demonstration of how *not* to do it, we'd have known that in the time it takes to swallow a couple of beers order would have been restored without any outside assistance at all.

The Skipper and I, as you'd expect, have had our fair share of groundings, although we started off our keelboat careers harmlessly enough. In our first boat we followed the policy common to most novices. That is, we were so concerned not to end up in trouble that we gave every rock, no matter how steep-to, such a wide berth that by the time we passed it, it was invisible below the horizon. It added a lot of sea time to our journeys and delayed quite a few evening meals to the point of midnight feasts, but at least we got there.

Our second boat, 'Marianda', tempted us into a more slaphappy frame of mind. She was a Fairey Atalanta with twin retractable keels, and when they were both wound firmly up into their housing, she could float in eighteen inches. Better still, if we did make a goof about depth, there was a fair chance that we could get away with it without our reputations suffering. Even if we met mud right outside the clubhouse we could fool the eagle-eyed audience by one of us (usually himself) staying at the tiller, smiling casually and keeping the sails filled, while the other nipped below for a bit of crafty cranking. Even solid rock didn't halt her, for the keels were designed to fold up like a penknife blade if they took a direct blow. True, at the next decent wave they would crash back down again with a second sickening thud but the shock was apparent only to those on board and we would charge on, shaken but unstoppable.

Indeed, 'Marianda' gave more concern to the innocent public than she ever did to her owners. If we thought a blow was coming, all we had to do to ensure a night's sleep was find a gently shelving beach, pick the tide right, crank up the keels and take her in at a run until she stranded herself. We might have the odd bump as the surf receded but after that we were as firmly lodged as a beached whale. This was fine for us, but many's the hapless child who has run screaming from his half-built sandcastle at the sight of our frothing bow-wave bearing down on him through the breakers.

The only snag was that it was hard to tell, from a distance, whether the chosen beach was gently sloping, steep, or had huge rocks or holes in it, and by the time you found out, it was too late to change your mind. Once, when a gale was making a Scottish anchorage untenable, we joined the cavalcade of bilge-keelers heading for the small drying pool at the head of the lough, duly grateful to Uffa Fox for the cleverness of 'Marianda's' design. Alas, the pool turned out to have a more uneven bed than we'd thought. The bilge-keelers on their sturdy little legs were fine, but we with our long flat hull

. . . ran screaming from his half-built sandcastle

encountered one of the larger rocks and 'Marianda' dried out
with her bows stuck up to the skies, as if she should have had an
anti-aircraft gun mounted on her pulpit. The Skipper and I lay
rigid in our bunks, not daring to move in case we upset the
equilibrium. The kids were less stoical and wakened us in the
small hours, gibbering with fright at finding themselves
crammed into the wet-locker, surrounded by clammy oilskins.

Sadly, this was not the last night we were to spend wishing
we'd been a bit more circumspect on our choice of anchorage.
There was the occasion when we holed up in an isolated pool,
with enough swinging room to accommodate a small fleet, and
settled happily to an evening's solitude and relaxation. As dusk

fell another craft nosed its way into our haven, and we were pleased to discover it was a pal we hadn't seen for some time. He dropped his hook at a safe distance and we had a shouted conversation, before making the clever decision that it might be fun to get a bit matier, and better still, we could achieve this without all the hassle of inflating dinghies. We would simply throw a line across, and then both pay out chain until we could bring the two boats alongside each other. There was no wind, and with both anchors lying well ahead, we thought there was little chance of any embarrassing tangle happening, and indeed it all worked out exactly according to plan and we shared an evening meal and cracked open a bottle or two.

On retiring at last to our respective bunks, the skippers decided that the squeaking of fenders between the hulls might be irritating so, having made sure we each had our full complement of crew, we made the seamanlike choice to cast off the warps and each lie once more to our own ground tackle. Unfortunately, nobody bothered to bring in any of the chain we had so carelessly paid out.

The first intimation that anything was amiss came a couple of hours later, when I realised I was a bit chilly and tried one of those snuggling, wiggling manoeuvres to bring the sleeping bag a little closer to nostril level, and found myself sliding with some speed across the vinyl before landing with a dull thud under the table legs. The blow caused the debris of the evening's merriment, till then maintaining its hold on the tabletop only by the stickiness of the spillages that had occurred, to start a movement of its own, and the Skipper was thrust into wakefulness by receiving a half-empty whisky bottle in the teeth, closely followed by a tinkling, clattering mêlée of crockery, glasses and dirty ash-trays.

There was nothing that could be done as our keel had already sunk well into the soft sand, so we wedged the kids firmly into their forward berths with lee-cloths and cushions and passed the rest of the night doing our overdue housework at an angle of 45 degrees.

Our pal had been luckier, and came on deck in the morning bright of eye after a secure night of refreshing sleep, to find the Skipper and me, tempers less than even, perched glumly on our upturned hull, and facing several more hours of the same before we could even prepare a hot breakfast. Feeling perhaps that it was a situation for which he was himself partly responsible – and, if asked, I'm darned sure the Skipper and I could have found evidence that the whole daft idea had been his in the first place – he wisely decided to forego the usual ribaldry.

One does learn – if slowly – by experience, and recently the Skipper and I had begun to hope that we were getting ourselves into sticky situations with less frequency. But last year in the Scilly Isles, whose anchorages we knew demanded close attention to detail, we proved yet again that overconfidence can be the sailor's enemy. Weary after a blustery passage from France, we were grateful to drop our hook in St Agnes' Cove, reputed to be good holding ground, and trot off ashore for a beer and a juicy Cornish pasty. Lolling on the grass outside the pub, we were suddenly brought to rigid attention by cries from the anchorage and the sight of our 'Mary Lunn' working her way purposefully backwards through the anchored boats, tugging jerkily at the chain hanging over the bow, like a terrier worrying a rat.

We leapt up in a flurry of crumbs and best bitter and made a run for her in the dinghy, clambering aboard, with perspiration flowing, just as her rudder touched the rocks. The Skipper fired the engine, which luckily responded to the urgency of the situation, while I, with the strength born of desperation, pulled like two men and a boy to get the hook up. At last it broke the surface, wearing a thick garland of weed and with a length of heavy chain wound firmly round its fluke. A lot of sobbing, grunting and several torn fingernails went into getting that lot clear and, by the time we were free, all we wanted was a secure lie and a sound night's sleep. We took quite a while to select our spot, stooging around the bay, peering down into the water, until I was sure I'd located a wide area of good, clear sand in which to place our faith. We anchored, gave her a hearty tug astern to be certain the hook was well dug-in, and allowed ourselves a small sigh of relief, before falling exhausted into our bunks.

We must have slept deeply because the first signals we received were the series of rhythmic, juddering bumps as the waves lifted and dropped our long keel onto the sand just before midnight. As I struggled to orientate myself and groped for the small torch under my pillow , a shaft of moonlight through the cabin window struck the Skipper's face with a weird, unearthly glow and the whites of his eyes, rolling warily to meet mine in the gloom, showed that he too had noted that all was not as it should be. Quickly pulling on sweaters over pyjamas, we huddled over the tide tables and conducted a brief, whispered argument about dates, times, rates of fall and just who should have made all these checks in the first place, and came to the worrying conclusion that we had at least two hours of tide to go, maybe more. Even as we reached this agreement, we realised that the bumping had stopped and 'Mary' was beginning to lean gracefully to port. Although the weather was calm and the bay quite sheltered, this was not a happy thought, as 'Mary Lunn' was built on traditional lines – long keeled, narrow-beamed, with a deep cockpit but not a lot of freeboard aft – and we had the uneasy feeling that, if she did go right over, she would fill up before she could right herself again.

Somehow we had to prevent this increasing heeling action but, with seven tons of wooden craft to support, remedies were not immediately obvious. Having deliberately picked our spot for its isolation and free swinging room, there was nothing solid nearby to get a line onto. We laid the kedge anchor and tried winching in on that, but we feared for our deckcleats and had to abandon the plan.

It was as the Skipper was rowing back in the dinghy that my bright idea struck me. If we could ram the rubber dinghy tightly in under the leeward side and lash it into place, it would serve as both cushion and flotation bag, minimising damage if we should start to pound in the waves and lifting her as the tide rose. Anyone who hasn't tried this should do so some time, strictly for entertainment value. We climbed into the dinghy and pushed it; we danced on it; we let some air out; we shoved again – and every time we got it vaguely into place and reached for a lashing, it wiggled, squeaked and, nimbly evading our clawing fingers, popped out again to frolic at the end of its string, mocking us.

Now both soaked to the skin, we rested and did a re-think,

Moodily watching the pre-dawn glow . . .

and it was the Skipper's turn to shine. What we needed, he decided, was some kind of leg to support us, so how about using the spinnaker pole? Brilliant, said I, and in no time we had it untied and lashed firmly to the main shrouds. But it, too, had a trick up its sleeve. Being pointed both ends, it could not offer a firm base whichever way we positioned it, but at every roll the lower end dug into the sand while the upper end slid up the shrouds with a blood-curdling squeal of metal against metal. Furthermore, it soon filled with water and as the stress came on, the pressure forced the water back up the pole and out of the numerous screwholes at the top, giving us lavish showerbaths we could well have done without. The kids, of course, slumbered peacefully through it all.

Finally, inspiration having run out, and the first waves beginning to lap greedily over the lower gunwale, the Skipper and I had to admit defeat. We climbed onto the weather deck, where at least our combined weight might do some good, and perched there, moodily watching the first pre-dawn glow creep into the sky. I must have dozed fitfully, for the next thing I knew was a sharp elbow digging me in the ribs and the bright light of the morning sun making my eyes water.

"Listen!" said the Skipper, excitedly. "Can you hear it?" I shook my head to banish the remnants of sleep and listened. . . and there it was, the same rhythmic thump, thump of keel against sand. 'Mary Lunn' was almost upright, and almost floating again. The whisky bottle bounced out of its locker and smashed on the floor. It was music to our ears.

We kept it to ourselves, of course. We didn't even tell the kids. We had a quick towel-down, sneaked back to our bunks for a couple of hours' recuperative kip, and when the rest of the anchorage awoke we were up there with the best of them, smiling gaily as we sampled the morning air.

"Sleep well?" enquired the skipper of a neighbouring boat, happily taking in the clear, calm day and the activity starting all around him. Without waiting for an answer he added, "You know, it's after a night like that that you realise what this cruising lark is all about!"

You do indeed.

4

And three's a crowd . . .

When you consider what an odd bunch we sailing types generally are, it's something of a wonder that we ever manage to form ourselves into working teams at all. Most crews I know are based more on a tolerance of each other's weird foibles than on a harmonious meeting of like minds. Having achieved this delicate balance, however, tipping the scales by indulging in musters, rallies and cruises-in-company must surely be a recipe for potential disaster that's matched only by holding a teenage disco in a room filled with antique vases.

Even a mini-cruise with a few selected pals can be dicey enough. It doesn't take too many navigational disputes or differences of opinion about suitable destinations for the inter-boat badinage to take on a cutting edge. And once you reach port, those slightly artificial gatherings may begin with good-natured argument about whose turn it is to lay on the festivities but can rapidly descend to more serious exchanges, with the skippers engaging in "I hate to say I told you so . . ." and "Of course, if you'd accepted my RDF fix in the first place . . ." cross-talk.

On one cruise we made with friends, I as navigator had quite a few altercations with my opposite number on the other boat about our position, which we resolved fairly amicably by splitting the difference and hoping for the best. However, when the lighthouse we'd been aiming for failed to appear on cue, the atmosphere cooled appreciably. Each privately blamed the other's sloppy thinking for the error and we talked on the VHF in clipped tones until I tried to avert a full-scale row by citing the poor visibility as responsible.

"After all," I said cautiously, "we can't see all that far. Maybe a few boat's lengths, at a rough guess . . ."

"According to my calculations," he replied with a smug, professorial air, "we have a visible distance of 1.27 miles, actually."

"Oh yeah?" I snapped back. "How did you work that out, then? Swim out with a long piece of string in your teeth, did you?"

Not every boat is greeted with unmitigated delight . . .

Three days later he was still explaining his methods to me with exaggerated patience, and I was still resolutely refusing to be impressed.

But at least, underneath it all, we remained friends. When the rally is on a much larger scale one has to face the inevitable fact that not everybody present may actually *like* everyone else. Not every boat is greeted with cries of unmitigated delight when it hoves into view at the appointed gathering spot, and though we may initially exchange thin smiles of tolerant resignation when the Hooray Henry with the detergent-bottle fenders, the eight-foot bowsprit and the dodgy engine appears, at the end of a week his effervescent humour may have begun to pall somewhat. As he comes creaming into port, the cheery groups exchanging chat on the already berthed craft disperse as if threatened by a volley of shotgun pellets. "Quick, get the dinghy alongside and for heaven's sake hide that bottle," hiss half a dozen skippers, suddenly remembering an urgent duty below decks. The newcomer is forced to flit from trot to trot like a questing honey-bee, and when he eventually grabs a set of guardrails and lurchs to a halt receives the same enthusiastic welcome accorded to a doorstep evangelist on washday.

Should he happen to be amongst the leaders on arrival, however, he'll find any number of craft willing to stand off and courteously offer him the inside berth – so that *he'll* be the one spilling soup into his lap as crew after crew, wash bags in hand, parade noisily across his coachroof and queue on the sidedeck for their turn at the ladder.

This business of crossing other people's boats can be a trial at the best of times. People never seem to make the trip singly, and no sooner have you recovered your balance from one set of heavy boots overhead than the next one is beginning its passage. On the lighter boats, this can set up such an alarming roll that the hapless diner, one arm thrust out protectively around his sliding plate and the other up in the air holding a slopping beer glass, is helpless to defend himself when the locker door behind him suddenly bursts open fetching him a stunning clout around the ear, followed by a succession of minor blows as he is buried in a deluge of coffee jars, sauce bottles and the contents of the fruit-bowl.

It's no better when it is your turn to make the crossing; however conscientiously you may take the tortuous foredeck route there is nearly always a cockpit picnic taking place whose participants cease their munching and eye you warily as you stumble your way through their maze of deck-fittings. You're torn between the necessary courtesy of exchanging a friendly greeting and the urgent need to watch where you're putting your feet – and it's no simple matter to maintain a warm social smile with your legs straddled painfully across two sets of twanging guardrails, or while extricating your boot from the face of the chap in the heads (where it has landed via an unnoticed open forehatch). At night it is even worse, for however lightly you may tread, sooner or later you'll encounter an almost invisible spinnaker pole and the resultant clatter,

coupled with your howl of startled agony, will have hatches thrown back and belligerent faces poking out like trapdoor spiders scenting prey.

The problem reaches its peak with the 'sunflower raft'. The Skipper and I were once part of a huge cruise-in-company which had one of these as its high spot. The idea is that a number of craft position themselves at equally spaced points of the compass and anchor themselves securely fore and aft. The remainder then tie onto them, gradually building up a complete circle of boats. It requires a fair degree of nerve and skill and is most impressive – if you happen to have a helicopter handy from which to view the effect. If you're a part of it, however, all you see is a forest of masts, a large number of highly apprehensive skippers, and a never-ending parade of heavy-footed revellers clutching bottles as they scramble from boat to boat.

In this gatecrasher's paradise, all attempts at civilised conversation were drowned out by the persistent thundering overhead, and it took a hard heart and a stern eye to turn away the questing faces popping up regularly in the hatchway, grinning in alcoholic bonhomie. There was some respite as large parties got under way on other boats. We could see the dark shapes of the funlovers as they clustered precariously on side decks and coachroofs, like oversized cormorants fighting for footage on an undersized rock. We did occasionally jump and spill our drinks as a sudden burst of exaggerated guffawing greeted the Commodore's latest witticism, but it was a small price to pay for the relief from continuously tramping feet.

We reckoned without the homeward journey however. As the various gatherings broke up, the well-lubricated revellers began the lengthy search for their own snug little bunks. Some would arrive on our sidedeck in threes, with two relatively upright chaps supporting a third, clearly tired and emotional and with limply trailing legs. Somehow we'd half-drag, half-roll him across the foredeck and on his way. Worse were the ones in whom the night's indulgences had stirred notions of bravado. One vaulted from the high bow of the boat next to us, and landed heavily on our anchor winch, requiring extensive first-aid before proceeding. Another grabbed handholds high in our shrouds and swung himself aboard Tarzan-style. His full-throated jungle yell was cut off abruptly as he failed to stop short of our boom and ended up lying across it kicking and spluttering, with eyes popping.

The ones who got the most sympathetic reception were the lost, lonely souls who'd probably been around the raft at least three times without finding home base. There would be a hesitant tapping on the coachroof and a timid voice crying, "Enid . . . Enid . . . Are you awake, dear?" We'd look out in time to catch a glimpse of a pale, blank face in the moonlight and a shape leaning at a dangerous angle over the guardrails before he'd miss his footing and tumble head-first into the cockpit.

"See? I *told* you I wouldn't be late back," he'd mutter as we struggled to untangle him from jib sheets and gear lever. Then, catching sight of the Skipper's unshaven features glowering at him in the gloom, he'd smile coyly and add, "Fancy an early night, sweetheart?"

To get the true flavour of the 'sunflower' though, you should be present at one of these rings of misplaced confidence when an unforecast blow arrives, especially in the middle of a dark night. Unless you're one of the fortunate few with your anchors down, it's a time to find out who your friends really are. Skippers, fuddle-headed from lack of sleep and with probably half their crew 'hors de combat' below decks, yell orders and throw off warps with panic-stricken abandon. Fingers with all the dexterity of a bunch of bananas stab desperately at engine controls, find forward instead of reverse gear and land their owners slap in the middle of the rapidly disintegrating circle with no room to manoeuvre and boats charging about blindly on all sides. Come the dawn, the boats are sited with all the precision of propaganda leaflets dropped from a speeding aircraft.

Mind you, there are those who respond with admirable calm

in such a crisis, no matter how self-indulgent the preceding hours. I heard of one skipper who leapt from his bunk, marshalled his crew and had his boat untied, repositioned and re-anchored with superb efficiency, even remembering to mount an anchor light before retiring to sleep it off. Rising for breakfast he thought it right to compliment the hands on their swift and seamanlike response, but was somewhat disconcerted to find a battery of unfamiliar eyes facing him suspiciously across the toast crumbs. "Well, well," he said heartily, "This is a bit of a surprise, I must say, but that was a fine job you did anyway, lads. Where is my regular crew, by the way?"

"Probably looking after *your* boat," replied their spokesman a trifle testily. "More to the point, where the hell is *our* skipper?"

On musters and rallies, a little inter-crew rivalry is bound to occur. When the chap in the white blazer and silk cravat charges through your cockpit bearing a wicker hamper filled with Fortnum's *pâté de foie* and champagne in bucket, it can be a bit galling if your lot happen to be swilling baked beans straight from the can at the time. Woe betide the husband who spends too much time in conversation with the nubile blonde in the brief bikini stretched out on the sundeck on the gin palace next door. "I fail to see why you find *her* so fascinating" snaps his wife, adjusting the sleeves of her stretch towelling playsuit tetchily, "She can't cook, and she doesn't know the first *thing* about navigation . . ." He'll get it in the neck later too. As the wind and tide rise and he lumbers from his snug bunk to adjust the shorelines before his trot becomes hopelessly enmeshed with the next, he'll meet her appalled gaze. "You're not thinking of going on deck like that are you?" she demands, eyeing with disgust his string vest and baggy pyjama bottoms. "I notice *he* wears monogrammed silk, and they don't gape either!"

Quite trivial annoyances in these crowded conditions produce manic behaviour at times. Take the halyard

question . . . to flap, or not to flap. Some love the sound of rhythmic tapping against the mast to lull them to sleep; others moan and ram pillows over their heads. At one muster we attended most of the boats on our trot were, like us, flappers by nature; but nevertheless every morning before raising sail we'd have to break our nails on a series of complex knots that had mysteriously festooned the rigging in the course of the night. We might detect the softest of foot falls on the deck above and, rushing up, even get a fleeting glimpse of a pyjama-clad rump disappearing in the surrounding blackness, but the Phantom Halyard Fanatic was never caught in the act and identified.

And that was no mean achievement, for keeping a secret of any kind is a virtual impossibility in this close-quarters living. If your neighbours don't get the unexpurgated highlights of your personal melodramas delivered with piercing accuracy by your kids, they can easily keep abreast of the nautical soap opera by lowering the volume of their own frank exchanges and tuning in to yours. Alerted by the crashing of locker doors, they smile knowingly as they pick up the voices through the adjoining hulls. "Well, if you spent more time on your own boat you'd know where things are kept. That's all *I* can say," announces a lady who plainly intends to say a lot more. "You see?" responds her man, probably addressing the auto-pilot, "I ask a simple question . . ."

Our last big cruise-in-company will probably be exactly that, if my opinion counts for anything, for it was such a chapter of accidents that it was enough to put anyone off the sport altogether. We set off for the Isle of Man, about thirty miles from home, in brilliant sunshine but had scarcely left the coast when a thick fog descended and what should have been a convivial jaunt became instead a dreary, isolated slog under engine with only the odd seagull and the occasional disembodied voice on the VHF to relieve the tedium. Retiring below for a rest from peering into the surrounding cotton wool, I drifted off into a doze but was rudely awakened by an angry bark from the Skipper. "For God's sake, if you're going to make tea, get on with it," he said irritably. "That damned kettle's been screaming for ages . . ." He broke off as he noticed my surprised look and the kettle, silent on an unlit gas ring. We scrambled up in time to see a wall of steel taking shape in the murk dead ahead, with a line of fascinated faces peering over the rails. It was a naval patrol boat which had presumably been giving us every warning signal it had before finally penetrating the hypnotic thundering of our trusty diesel. "Good thing, really," said the Skipper. "That'll keep us on our toes. Just you wait and see, it'll be plain sailing all the way now . . ."

And it was plain motoring anyway, until at last we picked out the misty headlands of the island and then closed together for our first port of call. We were pleased to see a large vacant mooring buoy in the bay, because not only would it absolve us from the anchoring routine but it would also give us the chance to try out the nifty little gadget we'd just acquired. It was one of those snap-hook jobs – tie it to your bow-line, slip it on the end of your boathook, clonk it over the ring and you're all secure in seconds. It worked a treat, and flushed with success we urged our fellow travellers to tie alongside to share a convivial lunch.

We were just relaxing nicely, and had sent a child to fetch out another couple of bottles, when one of the more alert types remarked that the mist must be clearing as the town buildings were becoming much plainer to the eye. So we learnt that while snap-hooks are magic for picking up a mooring they are not to be relied on for a more permanent attachment, especially not when several boats are tugging on them. There followed an undignified scramble as the Skipper rushed to the engine and I, for reasons unknown, frantically tried to jettison our companions. Their crews were not overjoyed by this display of self-preservation at all costs, and while those on the port-hand managed to get back to their boats in time, those on the other side were not so fleet of foot and would have had to watch their craft drift onto the rocks like a raft of Marie Celestes had not their yells of fury brought me up short as I was untying the last warp. So as the Skipper revved the engine to haul us off, I was forced to hang out precariously over the guard-rails trailing their precious craft behind on a flimsy length of line. With both arms being wrenched from their sockets it wasn't easy to maintain control and a sudden surge made them lurch in astern of us, clouting our pushpit and making it rear up from its mountings like a praying mantis.

Amid all the mayhem someone still had the presence of mind to take down the shipping forecast – which wasn't good. As our anchorage was a trifle exposed we decided to move round the island to a more sheltered spot on the other side, and clearly others had the same idea as we met flotillas all heading in the same direction and by the time we were berthed the trots were of a length that would have been pretty unstable in even the calmest weather. In fact it blew up to a full gale which crushed us against each other and the quay, while the swell rolling in round the breakwater had us all bucking up and down like fairground horses. Our planned evening of festivity degenerated into a miserable night of trial with all able-bodied crews passing the hours sitting in side-deck puddles with wellies extended to fend off our neighbours. There was precious little rest for anyone as shorelines twanged, rigging howled and overstressed fenders squealed like the souls of the damned.

So it continued well into the following day until, just as we'd snatched a lunch of doorsteps and cold tea, there was a slight easing in conditions. More sensible folk might have taken the opportunity to make a quick dash for home; but having come for a party we were darned sure we were going to have one, so we chose to use the lull to sample the hospitality of the local yacht club. This was an error. The children, fed up with being confined for so long, decided to give rein to their high spirits by holding running races up and down the lounge bar. On her second sprint, our own three-year-old athlete misjudged it and hurtled full-tilt into the wall, pole-axing herself in the process. There was a heartwarming rush to help, and in a very short time the casualty and I were speeding to hospital with sirens wailing. Luckily her injuries were more spectacular than serious but an overnight stay was ordered, just to be sure. I was briefly pleased by the thought of a night spent on terra firma; but I reckoned without the embarrassment of changing for bed. As I peeled off layer after layer of damp, fusty clothing preparatory to donning the hospital nightie (open down the back with ties one side only) I noticed the nurses turning away with an air of distaste, and ardently wished I'd had the foresight to change socks and wellies at least once in the preceding 36 hours. And as if this shame wasn't bad enough, every hour when they wakened my daughter for a routine check I would get a dim impression of loud voices and flashing torch-beams and lurch up rigid in my bed, clutching at the blanket and yelling for flares.

Meanwhile, back at the boat, the Skipper had his own problems as the gale returned with renewed fury. Left with only our seven-year-old as crew all he could do was double all warps, turn in and hope for a miracle. He might have got away with it had not the fishing fleet chosen that night to arrive back in port. Naturally they wanted the inner berths and were in no mood to trifle with pleasure-seeking yachties. One after another they appeared around the harbour wall, nudged in their bows and simply pushed until they were in their elected positions, extending the heaving trots until they almost reached the opposing shore. The swell was now running even higher, and the Skipper had to resign himself to yet another night of wakefulness, crouched over an engine thrusting full astern and fervently praying the diesel would outlast the storm.

When the wounded party and I returned to base in the morning the Skipper had given up the struggle and moved to a large metal buoy in the centre of the harbour. This was probably more secure, but as night fell – and the wind didn't – it too became untenable, for the steep seas rolling into the bay threw us around like a cork and we would repeatedly crash down onto the buoy, gouging out chunks of timber and sending a dolorous clanging through the boat. It was doing nothing for our daughter's throbbing head, and she saw no reason to keep the world in ignorance of her discomfort, which didn't help. Seeing the lights of the fishing fleet leaving the harbour, the Skipper decided it would now be a better bet to return to the relative shelter of the trots.

"Stand ready" he warned ominously. "We'll only get one chance at this!" Just as I cast off the mooring and he gunned her ahead, a large craft suddenly appeared from nowhere and charged straight across our bows. I watched in horror as our bowsprit bounced along her shrouds like a stick against the park railings. Somehow we got clear, but with the spar now pointing wildly to port. The big yacht meanwhile had smartly nipped in and pinched our privately designated berthing place. "Can't go back now!" yelled the Skipper. "Just grab hold of anything you can . . ." Frenziedly I scrabbled at her smooth topsides but as I finally got a tenuous grip on a length of toe-rail there was a blast of oily smoke from her engine and she roared away again, almost taking my grasping fingers with her.

"What the hell's going on?" I demanded of the crew of the next boat as I hurled ropes at them. Rapidly they hauled us in to their side and explained tersely, "Didn't want a big b. . . . . like that squashing us flat, did we? Told him to b. . . . . off." We sympathised, but clearly their words had not been heeded, as seconds later there was a splintering crash and the same big b. . . . . having completed his turn, slammed into our starboard side, ripping out a row of stanchions and a long strip of rubbing strake. It transpired that the crew were a team of total novices under training and, judging by the way they tried to use fender painters as mooring warps, hadn't got too far in the course. To ask them to move again would only have meant inviting trouble for someone else, so we settled for shuffling them to our inner side so that we could at least inspect our damage and remove any potentially lethal protrusions.

We had no time even to start this work, however, for we next became aware of a plaintive, frightened voice being carried to us on the wind's wailing. "Help! . . . Help!" we heard, and turned to see a dim masthead light describing an arc of nearly 180 degrees at the harbour entrance. It turned out to be a small boat which had been making a final run for port when a warp

"Hold on! I'm coming!"

had washed overboard and fouled the prop, so she was now drifting helplessly onto the rocks.

"Hold on! I'm coming," yelled the Skipper, leaping into our dinghy and pulling on the oars. I tossed him the end of our longest warp and began paying out as he surged away on the swell into the blackness. I was seriously worried now, as the dinghy was small and none too stable at the best of times, and the seas were large and unpredictable. The rope slackened and snatched in my grasp, and was getting heavier all the time. "For God's sake, don't just stand there! Give me a hand!" I snarled at the nearest novice.

"Right, right," he said, galvanised into something like action. "Here, give it to me . . ." Thus was that I nearly lost a husband, for he went on paying out rope until it ran out. Holding up the end for me to inspect he announced cheerfully, "Oh dear, it's not long enough. Still, never mind, he must be nearly there by now . . ." and so saying he prepared to jettison the last few feet overboard.

"Don't let go, you moron!" I screamed with little tact, but some accuracy. "Do you think he's taking that rope along for the exercise? Are we going to bring them all back by willpower or something?"

Fortunately at that moment there was a hail from the stricken craft that it was made fast, and we were able to make a concerted effort to heave her alongside.

The Skipper waved aside the gratitude and praise with a modest smile. He might have been less magnanimous had he known that the rescued crew would immediately abandon the boat in favour of the warmth and comfort of the local hotel and minutes later her stern warp would snap, allowing her to sweep round in an arc, breaking our bobstay and pulling a forward cleat clean out of the deck. This was the final straw as far as I was concerned, and I let forth a volley of abuse on sailing in general and my role in it in particular that amazed all present, before retiring to my bunk with a martyred expression and a bottle of Scotch.

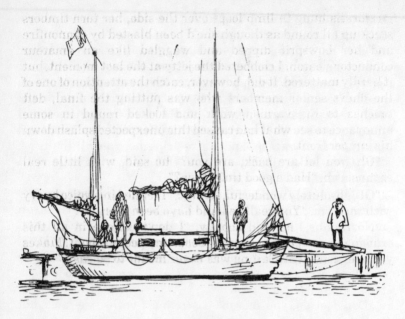

"Sailing was never meant to be easy."

The next morning the wind had died and, as we ploughed our weary way homeward, halfway across the Irish Sea the engine died too. The Skipper had to hang head down in the bilges while he located the fault and made an emergency repair which gave us a heady two knots for the rest of the trip. The reek of diesel did him no good at all and he succumbed to a rare bout of seasickness, so that when we at last nosed our way into our own club basin we were a sorry sight indeed. The Skipper, grey-faced and shivering, was slumped on a sail-bag in the cockpit; our daughter, puffy-cheeked and with one eye closed and blackened, sniffed tearfully as she clung tenaciously to my leg; our son, wearing his mutinous and put-upon glare was half-heartedly doing the deck work, while I, hollow-eyed and haggard, coaxed our bedraggled ship up to the pontoons. Her guardrails hung in limp loops over the side, her torn timbers stuck up all round as though she'd been blasted by cannonfire and her bowsprit dipped and waggled like an amateur conductor's baton. I clobbered the jetty at the last moment, but it hardly mattered. It did, however, catch the attention of one of the club's senior members who was putting the final, deft touches to his varnish work and looked round in some annoyance to see what had caused this unexpected splash down his jumper front.

"Oh, you lot are back, are you?" he said, with little real enthusiasm. "Had a good time, then?"

"Oh, absolutely wonderful, terrific," I replied in a voice heavy with sarcasm. "You really should have been there . . ."

"No thanks," he said shortly. "I don't believe in all this cruising in company nonsense. Too many people about. Makes you over confident. Sailing was never meant to be *easy*."

5

Hamming it up

With the ever-growing popularity of VHF radio, you'll find in any area where boats gather that the air waves are abuzz with inter-crew chatter, and not all of it of the clipped and formal type that goes with the acquisition of crucial nautical information. While skippers seek to justify the outlay of cash on the grounds that the radio is 'essential safety equipment', I can't help noting that a number of the conversations upon which I have shamelessly eavesdropped have not quite had the hairy-chested, deep-sea timbre one might expect.

For example, bounding around in a gale in Tobermorey harbour, we had our VHF ears flapping for exchanges about sudden changes of position, hoping thus to avert any potential disaster that could be heading our way. We thought we were onto something when we heard, as we flicked through the channels, a voice, authoritative in tone, asking, "Are you attempting to launch your dinghy then?" He came across as rough, masculine, maybe a trifle under pressure. Wow, we thought, this could be real red-alert stuff all right. Man overboard? Dragging onto the rocks? But then the voice continued, but somehow with less of an edge than before, as if the speaker were cringing inwardly at his own utterance. . . "Because Mary says if you're going ashore could you bring us another sliced crusty, half a dozen eggs and three more balls of her double knitting, in baby pink. . . "

Of course, it's part of the comradeship of the sea that we can perform little services like this for each other. Miss a vital weather forecast (and we all know how easy that is to do, even when you're trying) and you can do a quick radio search of nearby craft in the hope of finding one whose crew were not either asleep, or swilling duty-free, at the time. In practice, though, such information can be a bit dubious due to the understandable reluctance of the 'callees' to admit, in the presence of an unknown number of critical listeners, to the gaps in their knowledge.

"Nice of you to respond, 'Soothsayer'", intones the questioner heartily, "I was just wondering if you have the ten-to-six forecast?" "Er. . . we had rather a lot of static and I'm afraid we didn't quite catch all of it." (Sounds of clinking glasses and

". . . and three more balls of her double knitting, in baby pink."

immoderate laughter in the background cast some doubt on this explanation.)

"Oh yes, right, certainly, stand by," comes the reply, all brisk and seamanlike, an effect somewhat marred by his failure to remove his thumb from the 'transmit' button during the panicky consultation which follows. "The forecast, somebody give me the forecast quickly. What do you mean, you thought *I* was getting it? I distinctly told your mother to write it down. Honestly, even a simple task like that. . . Well, can't you give me even a rough idea?"

The hapless enquirer will probably wind up with a rapid re-hash of the lunchtime edition, or be fobbed off with a diplomatic lie. "Well, actually, old chap, my navigator feels the ten-to-six should be disregarded. This front seems to be moving in much more rapidly than the Met people expect. . . "

Any listening crews now face a dilemma. Should they interrupt this crosstalk with the correct version, thus making a fellow salt look a bit of an idiot? Or could it just be that 'Soothsayer's' navigator, assuming he/she exists, really does have some inside information? And, if so, maybe they should alter their own plans for the night? For this is one of the major drawbacks to radio eavesdropping. . . the kind of chatter exchanged by a couple of friendly skippers in an idle moment can quickly take on a new and alarming significance if half-heard by worried and inexperienced ears.

We had a fine demonstration of this in Crookhaven, a scenic and well-sheltered anchorage in County Cork. A large number of boats were anchored safely and well spaced out in the centre of the bay. Now dusk was descending, supper was over, and I was at the VHF, channel-hopping in search of entertainment. At the third click of the switch, I struck lucky.

". . . and, bearing that in mind," said a voice, seriously, "we really feel it would be a lot better to tuck ourselves in closer to the shore tonight. What do you think? Over."

At once, my skipper and I were exchanging worried glances. True, we had heard the forecast and there didn't seem to be anything unduly alarming in the offing, but on the other hand. . . well, if the wind were to go round just a little more to the south. . . you never knew. We turned up the volume control to get the reply.

"Yes, that seems like a very sensible move, 'Decisive'. You go ahead and we'll follow you over when you're settled."

We wasted no time in listening to any more. Space near the shore was limited and we'd have to get in quick to earmark a spot for ourselves, so our peaceful post-prandial snifter was abandoned for a spell of frenetic activity while we upped anchor and set off to claim our patch. It was no easy task, for all around us crews were engaged in identical toil, and it wasn't long before a dozen boats were milling about in the shallows, dropping our hooks across each other's chains, gasping at near-misses in the gloom, and exchanging meaningful glares with our nearest neighbours. We had to offer so many apologies that we decided to go ashore for a while to let the air of hostility cool, and it was there that we fell into company with 'Decisive's' crew and found out the truth. It transpired that they had managed to dunk their outboard engine during a bit of fishing from the dinghy, and all *they'd* been after was a shorter row to the pub.

It's quite surprising how many yatchsmen do fall prey to this 'herding' instinct, dodgy as it is; especially when you find at the last minute, as we did, that the boats you're so enthusiastically tailing are all bilge-keelers heading for a quiet squat on the mudflats, while you're a fin-and-skeg that needs six feet and has only got five and a half.

Try sailing around the Scilly Isles to see the herds a-wandering. These lovely islands lie at the convergence of no fewer than four sea areas, so getting a correct interpretation of the weather forecast is even more than usual a matter of intelligent guesswork. Moreover the popular havens, though each with its own merits, also have the disadvantage of offering at least one quarter open to the prevailing winds and seas. To get a comfortable lie each night it is necessary to port-hop with some regularity. After a dubious forecast, the grey waters will be dotted with questing craft, all heading for different spots in an earnest search for peace of mind, while the airwaves hum with nautical radio hams offering conflicting advice, false assertions of confidence, needless doubts and instilling mild feelings of panic.

"Well, we're going for Old Grimsby," I announced to a friend who'd called to enquire one threatening evening. "They say the holding's good and we'll get some extra shelter when the tide falls and the reefs are exposed. . . "

"No, no, *we're* heading into *Old* Grimsby," he replied. "We're going to nip in below the castle, out of the tide. You must be going for *New* Grimsby."

Before I could argue a new and officious voice cut into our discussion. "Actually, Cromwell's Castle is at *New* Grimsby," he informed us. "And with this wind, I'd say it was *definitely* the safest place to be."

Our pal did not take kindly to this. "In that case," he said with some dignity, "we have just arrived in Middle-Aged Grimsby, because *I'd* say the safest place to be would be sitting under a tree."

Others were then anxious to join the debate.

"If you worried, there's lots of space up here in Tean Sound. We're tucked in behind some fishing boats, snug as a bug. . . "

"There isn't a *ripple* in Helen's Pool. . . "

"Wouldn't Porthcressa be a much better bet. . . ?"

And so it went on until we'd all made our choices and settled down. And it blew all right. We heaved and bounced at the end of our chain but fortunately held our position. Not so the boat ahead of us, which dragged anchor, sideswiped us in passing and went hard aground. As this news was relayed, we were the centre of a barrage of concerned VHF voices, all unable to help but wishing to be kept up to date with events. Scarcely had we got this problem under control when the wind veered, we swung over the shallow patch and it was then our turn to touch bottom.

I felt a strong temptation to break into a song-and-dance routine.

Re-anchoring in a howling gale and pitch darkness is no fun task, so we called to our still-grounded friends to put on their navigation lights so we could at least avoid adding to their troubles by blundering into them. Instantly, our whole anchorage became a veritable fairyland of red, green and white dots, while I, struggling on the foredeck, was blinded by the converging beams of half a dozen powerful spotlights, all eager to light my way. I felt a strong temptation to break into a song-and-dance routine.

It is often quite an effort of nerve to make that initial call to a strange craft. It helps, for a start, if the name is easy to catch. Around our own Irish yachts, with their fondness for the Gaelic tongue, you see names that could be pronounced in a variety of ways, none of them the one you've stumbled through. My skipper once took a call from a boat whose name sounded remarkably like 'Gongonzola'. He found an easy way of dealing with that. He whipped round and shoved the microphone into my hand. "It's for you!" he said, shortly, and disappeared up on deck.

Mind you, the name could very well have been correctly heard, for there are a lot of daft names about. And the fact that you are required to repeat your choice three times as a call-up routine doesn't help. I saw a boat recently which was named 'Woof', and no doubt its owners have excellent reasons for their selection, but one can't help imagining the mayhem when they take to the air.

"This is yacht 'Woof', 'Woof', 'Woof'. . . "

"Down, boy!" "You don't frighten me, sir!" . . . "Tell that dog to use a working channel!" and so on. It must become tedious, to say the least.

Or how about "Port Hamble, Port Hamble, this is 'Desperate', 'Desperate', Desperate'". You wouldn't know whether to call back or launch the lifeboat.

Put them in pairs and it gets better. "'Jail-Bird', 'Jail-Bird', this is 'Bloodhound', 'Bloodhound'" . . . or "'Bambi', 'Bambi', this is 'Deerhunter'".

We have two local boats named 'Kiss-Kiss', and 'Give-us-a-Cuddle'. When they start broadcasting together it fair brings a blush to a maiden's cheeks.

But then, that's your own fault for listening in in the first place. We shouldn't, but we all do, and it certainly beats *The Archers* for entertainment value. Some of us seem to have a talent for it. We once watched as a small yacht with an obviously novice crew tried repeatedly and unsuccessfully to anchor in the exact spot they'd chosen for themselves. Over and over again they circled round, hesitated and then dropped the hook, and each time they dragged back just a little too far, until their stern was bobbing only feet from the bows of the craft behind them. The skipper of the wronged craft divided his time between nipping up to the bows to stare them into submission and nipping back to the radio to drop another little gem into the ears of his fascinated audience.

"If at first you don't succeed . . ." he gave us at the start. Then "If you can keep your head when all about you are losing theirs and blaming it on you . . ." Then, as they appeared to admit defeat and head off to a new patch, we got "I wandered, lonely as a cloud . . ." and finally, as that questing bow swung once more into his line of vision, "We have returned. . . 'Blessed are they that hunger and thirst after righteousness' . . ."

It was fortunate for them that they were too busy to hear, for one can all too often have cause to regret, rather than relish, the yachtsman's habit of tuning in to private conversations. I have to confess that I have suffered in this manner myself.

One year, we, in our yacht 'Mary Lunn', were sailing in company with another boat from our club, and at the end of the long haul from Ireland were rapidly closing with the Brittany coast – but how rapidly, and with which part of the coast, was not entirely clear. We'd run into a thick mist some time previously, and despite lengthy and heated arguments about distances run and RDF fixes, had no really accurate idea of where we were.

As we motored cautiously onwards, straining our eyes to catch a glimpse of anything identifiable, the dim outline of a large French naval vessel appeared through the murk. Our pal at once tried to contact her on the VHF but several calls, in English but with a strong Northern Ireland accent, failed to get a response.

"Hey, Les," he grunted sulkily at last. "You're supposed to be our linguist. Try some of your Gallic charm on him."

My reputation as a linguist was based on shaky foundations. I'm a fair mimic and so can produce a quite convincing French accent but the sad truth that I lack the basic vocabulary to say anything at all useful was one I had so far kept successfully hidden. I'd even fooled myself.

"No problem," I said, brimming with confidence, and I'd opened the channel and launched into my spiel before realisation dawned that I hadn't a clue how to continue.

"Allo, allo. . . er, French warsheep, French warsheep *ici* yacht 'Marie Loon', 'Marie Loon' . . ." Despite some impressive

"Allo, allo . . . er, French warsheep . . ."

rolling of the r's and a few strangled vowel sounds, I'd managed only one word of the language so far. I ploughed on, frantically searching my memory for the right words for 'lost in the fog'.

"*Nous* . . . um . . . *nous* come from Irelande. *Nous sommes perdus dans le brouillard* . . ." There, that was better, but instead of the calm statement of fact I'd hoped for it had come out as a pathetic, nasal whine, like a nervous ten-year-old auditioning for *Babes in the Wood*.

"We want . . . I mean, *voulez-vouz* give us our poseetion, *s'il vous plait?*"

As I waited, sweat beginning to trickle from my armpits, there was a burst of static followed by a burst of rapid-fire French, totally incomprehensible to me apart from a repeat of the words 'Marie Loon'. It was clear that I'd established contact, but equally clear that it was going to be no help whatsoever unless some common ground could be found, and fast. Cursing, not for the first time, my tendency to let my tongue run on ahead of my brain, I had to capitulate.

"I'm so sorry. I didn't quite catch that. I wonder, could you possibly speak in English?"

He turned on his mike just a little too early to spare me his swift snigger of amusement. "Ah yes, but of course, Madame. I theenk eet will make life just a leetle easier for us all, yes?" And he gave us our fix in precise and grammatical BBC English that would have put Angela Rippon to shame.

"Oh, *merci, monsieur*," I gabbled weak-kneed relief in every syllable. "*Merci*, very much indeed."

With one last vain attempt at bravado, I called up our pal. "There you are, you see? It's easy when you know the lingo . . ."

But he was too hysterical to care.

6

The inhuman race

Racing, so the devotees assure me, is the really serious side of the sport. Nerve, gear and iron resolve are given the ultimate test, and there's no room for relaxed enjoyment and a giggle or two. If so, I'm glad to see that there are a few brave cruising types willing to do their bit to bring some light relief, as was demonstrated recently at the start of the Whitbread Round-The-World event. As the finely tuned craft thundered back and forth, jockeying for position on the line, the TV camera switched to the weary face of a race official, megaphone pressed to tight lips. "Yacht X, Yacht X," he intoned in a voice heavy with threat, "if you do not immediately clear the area, this race cannot start!" The shot changed to an aerial view of the mayhem that was the starting line. Vast, expensive boats, each apparently crewed by twenty oilskinned gorillas, creamed past each other with inches to spare, and there, in the very centre of it all, bravely battling the wrong way, was a small family cruiser complete with rubber dinghy on a long line astern. The husband, with a look of supreme panic on his face, was thrusting his tiller this way and that in an effort to avoid collision while the wife, knuckles white as she clung on to the cockpit seat, was clearly keeping up a running tirade of the "Watch out! Look behind you! Oh God, here comes another one!" type. It was as if a Morris Minor had suddenly found itself in the middle of Le Mans.

I felt for that family as soulmates, for I too am a cruising sailor by nature and the racing scene is alien ground to me. Logging an impressive nautical mileage, exploring remote anchorages, meeting the challenges of living aboard for weeks on end – all these to me have more significance that the racing man's world of flags, protests, handicap ratings and all the other self-imposed trials involved in being first across the finishing line.

Unfortunately for me, one of the conditions of membership of our yacht club is that all club boats will turn out and show their competitive spirit from time to time. Actually getting us to the starting line is another matter, as excuses can always be found. In light airs, it's futile for us to show ourselves as our boat just does not perform without a good weight of wind. Give us a hearty breeze, and I point out that our classic craft is not in full

racing trim and it would be foolhardy to risk her hard-to-replace gear merely to gain a few marks on a score sheet. Anything in between, and it's ideal cruising weather and I'm afraid we'll be away all week-end, but thank you for asking. Let them spring the ultimate persuader – that it's only by racing her that you really get to know your boat – and I'm ready with the final riposte, that it's only by cruising that you really get to know yourself.

The truth is I find racing expensive and terrifying, and I can't understand the rules no matter how hard I try. In truth, I don't try all that hard, but I did once buy a book on the subject. I ran to 150 totally baffling pages and included a very short section, designed for idiots, on 'Rules That Everyone Should Know'. I couldn't even make head or tail of that. Faced with instructions such as 'At a windward mark, if on opposite tacks, take the mark away and apply the principles as if in open water (Rule 42.1c and 36)' I find that the normally agile brain becomes instantly sluggish and befuddled, probably because my own principles when in open water stick at survival at all costs, and women and children first.

My Skipper, although often heard to maintain that the true joy of sailing lies in escaping from the rules inflicted by authority, is much more ready to pick up the racing gauntlet than I. Not so long ago he was mustard-keen to be numbered among the offshore hot-shots and offered himself as crew at every available opportunity. To find out why these offers were snapped up with ever-diminishing frequency, we have only to look a little more closely at his actual performances under test conditions.

His first outing, an overnighter around the Isle of Man, seemed promising. Joining a hefty, well-practised and well-organised crew, he was told to bring just himself, a bare minimum of spare clothing and a contribution (financial) towards the food for the team. It came as something of a shock to find that the hard tack provided for this fee was well below his personal idea of starvation rations and – worse still – that

The racing scene is alien ground to me.

the consumption of alcohol was banned for the duration of the trip. Luckily for him, but perhaps less happily for the would-be record breakers, I took the precaution of secreting a large fruitcake and a generous flask of grog in his rolled up long-johns. Coming on watch in the middle of the night, the owner was less than thrilled to discover my hero, incandescent from some inner fire, carolling merrily to himself as he surfed down the breakers with scant regard for the designated compass bearing, in a cockpit liberally spattered with squashed sultanas.

He made a stern resolution to be less self-indulgent on his second offshore venture which was, not entirely surprisingly, on a different craft. He behaved impeccably until in the first grey light of dawn, only a few miles from the finish, the wind dropped completely. With the boat going nowhere and the sails idly slatting back and forth, my Skipper and his fellow foredeck heavy found time dragging a bit and so decided to enliven the waiting hours by swapping jokes of a highly unsavoury nature. They were quite discreet about it, but they hadn't reckoned on the fact that the section of crew at rest in the forecabin beneath their feet were also listening in. So when my man delivered the punchline of a particularly risqué favourite it provoked not just a sly, subdued sniggering, but a chorus of mast-rattling guffaws.

The owner made the journey from helm to foredeck in one furious bound, and was quick to pinpoint the culprit. "How *dare* you laugh on my boat!" he screamed. He shook an angry fist at the silent, unmoving world. "Don't you realise that conditions like these demand *supreme concentration?*"

Perhaps he was right, for they eventually went on to win the race, albeit in a hostile silence with the owner playing huffy headmaster to my skipper's sheepish schoolboy.

Mollified by this success and being of a forgiving nature – or perhaps just short of crew – the owner offered a repeat invitation for the following weekend. This time it was blowing hooligans and a very demanding beat ensued, during which my man pulled out all the stops to please, ending up on the weather deck, shoulders firmly lodged in the shrouds and boots dangling over the side. There, exhausted by his labours, he inexcusably drifted off into a deep and dreamless sleep. It says much for his indispensable qualities as a crewman that everyone forgot he was there – even when the boat slammed over onto a different tack. He received the rude awakening of being thrust, head-first, into the turbulent waters of the chilly Irish Sea. His language was a trifle immoderate and he was not asked back a third time.

I can't say I wasn't relieved. It wasn't the danger that bothered me – after all, cruising is not to be undertaken lightly either – but I have seen the effect the racing bug can have on a grown man and I don't like it. I have a friend, funnily enough a nautical publisher by trade, who's normally a brisk, go-getting executive type with no obvious weaknesses of character. But

. . . head-first into the Irish Sea.

mention racing and the nostrils flare, a manic gleam enters the eye and even his breathing speeds up. He makes it his mission to keep me abreast of what's new on the racing scene and his stories never fail to astound me.

I hadn't realised, for instance, that merely *owning* a boat is no guarantee that you'll actually go sailing on her. Once, his owner was delayed five minutes parking the Rolls (which in itself is an indication of the bare minimum of wealth required to be part of this unhappy breed) and arrived at the quayside to find that his crew, anxious not to be late at the line, had pushed off without him. And when on board, so I'm reliably informed, the owner may find he has nothing to do other than listen to complaints and sign cheques, as even he must prove his worth at a job or relinquish it to somebody with better qualifications. I can just see my own Skipper accepting *that* with good grace!

I don't think he'd take too kindly to the abandonment of his creature comforts either, for despite the hairy-chested image he likes to project he's much addicted to the cushion-behind-the-head, steak-pie-in-the-oven style of passage-making. My pal tells me it's all very different on the racing front. A pukka offshore boat may have fittings every few feet and winches the size of garden sundials on deck, but down below it's as bare and sparse as a punishment cell with only a stuttering paraffin stove and a bucket-and-chuck-it loo to meet the crew's most basic needs, and probably not even that.

I was intrigued to learn that other traditions have been overthrown in the search for maximum efficiency. The change-of-watch routines that have served generations of seafarers well over the centuries are apparently no longer good enough for the racing boys. The idea that, at designated times, the entire on-watch crew retires and a completely new bunch takes over leads, they claim, to periods of confusion when, perish the thought, the boat doesn't go as fast as it should. The oncoming watch are bleary-eyed and sluggish, don't know where they are, and in the desire to keep up the honour of their particular regiment immediately begin changing everything. The gang going off-duty don't help, their sole desire being to hit the sack as rapidly as possible. So now, it's the 'buddy' system that's in vogue. If I've understood it correctly, what happens is that the entire crew form themselves into pairs, and these 'buddies' decide between them on a system of watch-keeping that suits them personally. They may elect to do their change-over every four hours, or six, or two, in fact whatever turns them on, and they keep to this pattern for the duration.

In theory, this all sounds very fine, as the watch then changes at staggered intervals and some sort of continuity is preserved, but I wonder how well it works out in practice. I mean, when your entire team is struggling into oilskins and getting ready to take its turn, it would be a strong man who could cling mutinously to his sleeping bag and refuse to budge. But when it's only the wrath of your buddy you have to contend with, I can see all sorts of petulant battles of will taking place in the chilly small hours.

"Oh come on . . . just another hour, please? I'll make it up to you, I swear I will . . ." "But we *agreed*. . . honestly, if you can't trust your *buddy* . . ."

Mind you, it has to be said that we family crews have used similar methods of bribery and threats for years and we seem to get by, most of the time.

Of course, if you're really competitive, you don't think of rest at all, and going off-watch merely means that you move from the cockpit to the side deck, where you spend the 'free' time serving as human ballast. It's hardly surprising that this lack of revitalising sleep can sometimes lead to frayed tempers all round, and the emergence of the mean streak that is part of the racing mentality. For there is, my friend once whispered to me behind his hand, a 'dirty tricks' brigade who will stop at nothing to gain a yard or two. To give but one example, although it is illegal to actually put out one's navigation lights when racing at night, *some* sneaky types have been known to fit dimmer switches to the controls so that the lights can be faded gradually, at will. The idea is that the leading boat, watching his nearest rival apparently falling slowly behind in the chase, may relax his guard enough to let the blighter creep past in the gloom. Hardly sporting, chaps, surely?

In a vain attempt to enthuse me with his obsession, my friend took me one evening to Lymington Marina, so I could feast my eyes on the very boat on which he lives out his fantasies. Unfortunately, she wasn't there. After the build-up to this treat that I'd received on the way, I thought the sudden anti-climax might prove embarrassing for him, but not a bit of it. "This," he breathed in awed reverence, waving an expansive arm to indicate the bare pontoon and the patch of grey water alongside, *"This* is where she normally lies. . . " For once, I was at a loss for words.

He didn't notice, though, for he was off again, this time having spotted a huge, sleek Admiral's Cup contender lying a few pontoons away. She was, even to my jaded eye, quite magnificent, but even so I'm glad there was nobody about to witness the air of hushed worship my pal then adopted. He stroked her guardrails, he fondled her winches and at last, unable to resist her allure any longer, sneaked aboard to sit behind the wheel, leaning back, bracing himself against imaginary seas, eyes closed in ecstasy. You could almost hear him murmuring 'Brrrrm. . . brrrrm' like a sort of nautical Toad.

You don't even need to be in his league for the rot to set in. At our own small club, those who would immediately abort plans for a short sail and a picnic at the first hint of drizzle will gleefully set out in gales or a torrential downpour if there's a race on. People whose cars haven't seen a wash leather all year will dry out their craft twice monthly and laboriously scrub off microscopic specks of weed and barnacle that might 'inhibit their performance'. Folk who gripe endlessly about forking out their annual subscription will replace blown-out spinnakers with a cheerfulness that is not unmixed with pride.

These people seem to feel that it's part of the great crusade to draw others into the same insanities. Over the season we run a series of Lifeboat races, to raise money for that worthy cause, and it's no use hoping to get away with just a donation, no matter how generous. Eternal shame awaits any keelboat still on her mooring when the starting gun sounds. Even I am obliged to venture out – though my presence may not be immediately obvious to the onlooker, as all that scrapping for position at the line gives me the cold shivers. I try to persuade the Skipper to hang back behind the field and catch up later – admittedly an unlikely event. Failing that, as the close-quarters stuff gets going, you'll find me down below on a bunk, huddled into a foetal position and clutching a life-jacket.

Once we're off, it's the wheel all the way for me, as our boat's biggest sails are too much for me to handle under pressure, or that's my story anyway. The truth is I do have a tiny competitive urge buried somewhere about my person, which emerges as soon as the fleet fans out and my confidence builds. Under normal conditions, my steering is devoted to keeping the

"Leave him! Leave him! This is a race!"

boat sailing as near vertically as possible but, when racing, I'll have her charging along on her ear, gunwale under, kids hanging on grimly by their fingernails and the Skipper with a grin like a split sack.

He is always cheerfully optimistic when racing, at first anyway. If we happen, by some fluke, to be pointing in the right direction when the gun blasts, it's "Do you realise we could actually *win* today?" Then, as the rest of the fleet begins to show its paces, we get, "Keep her going. We've got a good handicap, remember!" Gradually, a note of realism intrudes. "Well, if we get a fast leg downwind, at least we shouldn't be last..." until finally, with a sigh, it's "Never mind, as long as we beat old Fred I'll be happy." Old Fred is the owner of the only other large wooden boat in the club that is rated akin to ours

The Cup . . . takes a prohibitively expensive amount of champagne to fill it.

and these races usually wind up as a ding-dong battle between us, mostly won by Fred and his demon spinnaker. But then he has a larger and more mature family than ours, and also seems to regard them as expendable. Last time out, this monster sail of his, garishly striped in black and yellow, suddenly filled while two of his lads were still holding on to the tack and clew and just as Fred made an abrupt change of course. They were lifted high off the deck and then plummetted down again, his son-in-law landing heavily astride the guard rail (which can't have done Fred's grandfatherly prospects much good) and his son going smack into the tide. As the boat careered on like a demented wasp and Mrs Fred attempted some smart rescue work with a boat-hook, the devoted father could be heard screaming, "Leave him! Leave him! This is a race!"

Our own spinnaker work is a great deal more cautious, if it happens at all. We more often employ the safer tactic of breaking out our trusty mizzen staysail, a novel example of the sailmaker's art striped diagonally in a tasteful combination of red, blue, green, orange and purple. It does nothing at all to improve our sailing performance, but we can sometimes gain a second or two over the other craft as they stop to stare in disbelief or manoeuvre closer to deliver wisecracks. "What's all this then? Stop me and buy one? We'll have two vanilla cornets and a raspberry ripple. . . "

In the end, we count the day a triumph if we manage to make it back to the clubhouse in time to hear the applause that concludes the prize-giving. That we're never to be called to the dais to receive the winner's plaudits brings us no great distress. The Lifeboat Cup is very big one, and it takes a prohibitively expensive amount of champagne, or for the hard men in our club, Irish whiskey, to fill it. Success may be sweet, but the skipper and I prefer to reserve our hard-earned cash to buy bonded stores – the next time we go cruising.

7

Heavy petting

There are times at our yacht club when the casual visitor might be forgiven for thinking he'd strayed into the arena at Crufts. Indeed there have been occasions, or so the Commodore once testily informed me as he wiped his wellie on a handy tussock of grass, when the dogs have outnumbered the people present by about two to one.

This may have been a slight exaggeration, but it does seem to be true that an increasing number of us, reluctant to face either the kennel fees or the puddles on the kitchen floor that result from leaving our pets behind, are bringing the little dears along to join in our sailing exploits – as if life weren't difficult enough.

Mostly our animal pals are dogs, although one young couple were brave enough to appear with a small kitten. It gambolled very prettily on the foredeck and provoked a lot of clucking and cooing from passing enthusiasts as they lay alongside the jetty; but once the ship took to sea it was a different scene. Unnerved by the sudden instability of its environment, the moggy showed a mad desire to scramble up anything that seemed to represent security and human contact. Staggering ashore, dripping blood and fur, the proud parents bunged the cat in the car, its nautical career at an end before it had really begun.

We dog-owners were a bit disappointed about this, because

for a while our motley collection of mutts had called a halt to their normal hostilities and united under the flag of truce to see off this feline intruder. Now the threat was past, they were happy to return to the antisocial pursuits that had occupied them previously – overturning rubbish bins, consuming the contents and anything else they could get their thieving jaws into, and then jettisoning the results, at will, on bunks, cockpit soles or the clubhouse lawn; conducting sudden snarling fights under the feet of contentedly chatting groups causing the more nervous members to leap onto chairs and hurl jugs of water about; forcing their unwanted romantic attentions on sail-bags, small children and, just occasionally each other; howling half the night and, of course, cocking their collective legs on anything that stayed still long enough. Our own hound achieved the ultimate award for this one, by actually piddling over the Commodore's foot while I was talking to him.

Yachting dogs show as much variety (and eccentricity) of character as their human counterparts. Take Wellington,

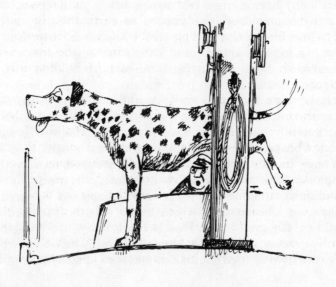

the wire-haired dachshund, who is high on pedigree but low in centre of gravity. He's a seasoned old salt, but his stunted legs lack the necessary 'oomph' to get his portly body from pontoon to deck level; so he has to sit forlornly by the boat, baying like a wounded bull, until someone notices him and lifts him aboard. As he's given to nocturnal wanderings, it can mean sleepless nights for his hapless owners, and for nearby crews. It's a good thing he doesn't try it at sea because, on the odd occasions he has fallen in, his peculiar bodily construction has meant that it's a matter of pure chance which way up he floats.

Or there's Mitzi, a tiny Yorkshire terrier who, being just the right size to fit neatly into an oilskin pocket, would at first seem to be the ideal boat dog. Once on board, though, she has a mania for climbing into lockers and hiding herself in their shadowy depths. Anyone unwise enough to grope inside for tomato ketchup or a clean pair of socks is rewarded by a savage growl and a set of teeth like a sprung gin-trap.

At the other end of the size range, we have Magill the St Bernard, gentle as a lamb, but whose very bulk represents a problem. Fortunately his owner has a large boat, but nevertheless is often asked where on earth the dog sleeps. "Anywhere he damned well pleases" is the rueful response.

Biggles *looks* as though much the same sentiments would prevail with him. He's a fearsome-looking bulldog with a belligerent undershot jaw from which a row of gnarled teeth protrude. He's a dog to smile timidly at from a discreet distance, but if you do he rolls on his back, slobbers affectionately and begs to have his tummy tickled. He does keep the boat free of unwelcome interlopers, though.

Which is more than can be said for our own canine companion. For reasons which defy analysis, we go in for Dalmatians, and our first – Fletcher – displayed a degree of uselessness aboard ship which could only be matched by another of the same breed. He was large, noisy, ate massively, drank to excess, was seasick, clumsy and could be violent when provoked (we've had human crew who displayed similar failings, it's true, but not all at once). He was, in fact, more than sixty pounds of extra baggage that any family cruiser could well do without, but to leave him behind would have caused mutiny amongst the junior crew, so he became a fixture, despite all the additional burdens his presence caused for the senior partners.

Not only were the bunks, sweaters and sleeping bags, saucepans and crockery – even the navigational instruments – covered with a fine overcoat of white hairs, but there were also the not inconsiderable problems of where he'd sleep, how he'd be fed and watered and where and how he'd answer his depressingly frequent calls of nature. A big dog has big needs and Fletcher caused us a great deal of trouble (and embarrassment) through his urges to dispose of what we had so laboriously stowed, prepared, and fed into him. His initial cruise with us was aboard 'Polmarah', a converted pre-war fishing smack of generous proportions. He came aboard with many misgivings, viewed the available accommodation with much disdain, selected the pilot berth nearest to the warmth of the engine as being his by divine right, and settled down to sleep away his first night passage. I cannot, even now, find any satisfactory reason why I decided on leaving the quayside to boot him out of this snug nest to partake of a fine, hearty meal but a couple of bumpy hours later I had cause to regret my ill-timed caring instinct. A frantic battering of steel-tipped paws against my legs and a pair of desperate brown eyes pleading with me in the gloom drove the message home.

"That's OK" said the Skipper cheerily as I relayed the news. "Let him come up on deck. We can just sluice it down. . . Oh, my God!"

The wheel was left spinning wildly as we both made a dive for the dog's tail, disappearing through the guard rails. "You damn fool!" muttered the boss through clenched teeth, leaving some doubt whether he was referring to me or the dog, who was now, with nose brushing the wave-crests, struggling manfully to go into reverse gear.

The experience left its mark. On the plus side, it produced in the animal a remarkable capacity for self-control which he demonstrated most ably later in the cruise. Riding out a gale, we found that tide and weather had produced conditions so choppy that it would have been foolhardy in the extreme to attempt to load a five-stone dog into a gyrating rubber dinghy to take him ashore. So Fletcher was forced to remain aboard, with legs tightly crossed, for a period of thirty-five hours with only the odd tortured whine of complaint. When he did reach the slipway, we were almost washed off our feet by the flood he unleashed.

On the debit side, however, Fletcher developed the habit of taking opportunities to do his unleashing as and when they occurred, and this was frequently when we were tied up alongside other boats, their foredecks being his most favoured spot. He would disappear on a tour of the neighbouring craft, while their unwitting crews offered friendly pats and titbits. Having selected the one with the most immaculate teak-laid decks and the most carefully coiled jib sheets, he would pause, deposit mightily, and then trot happily home, relief in every step. How many times have we been called to account by a discreet tapping on the coach-roof, a polite clearing of the throat and, "Er, that's a most interesting dog you have there. I presume you *do* carry a bucket and brush aboard. . . ?"

Of course, it's always the Skipper who gets the job of clearing up. Indeed, he's not slow to point out that, despite the nauseating babytalk that assaults his ears during doggy playtimes, when it comes to 'walkies' on a wet night volunteers to take 'Oozums-woozums' ashore are in short supply. Other boats seem to have the same rules. Look around any popular anchorage on a typical British summer evening and you'll see the dinghies going away, skipper oilskinned against the lashing rain, hunched resentfully over the oars, while the family hound stands erect and eager in the bows, a weird canine figure-head with eyes fixed glassily on the far horizon. As the tender pulls away from the mother craft there is often a

Struggling manfully to go into reverse gear.

female cry from the companionway: "I know they're still open, and I'm putting your cocoa on the gas NOW!"

Getting a dog to climb into the dinghy in the first place can be a trial, and when conditions were blustery and the dog a neurotic and excitable Dalmatian it became an epic undertaking. Neighbouring crews often gathered on their side decks to watch us at work. The skipper, supposedly the strongest of us, would climb into the dinghy and brace himself, feet apart, knuckles white on the guard rail, ready to receive the load. The children would be stationed at strategic points about the deck to cut off any attempt at retreat and I would grab the dog's collar and get ready to give a hefty shove at the critical moment. Fletcher's eyes would take on a wild and haunted look, his claws extended searching for a grip on the slippery deck, and he would begin a plaintive whimpering. "That's all right, boy," we'd croon encouragingly at the start. "Come on now, there's a good lad . . ." This would degenerate into "For heaven's sake MOVE, you b. . . . idiot!" as time passed by. Finally, with the air of a suicide leaping from a tower block, Fletcher would hurl himself forth. One foot would land on my husband's chest, another in his mouth, while the remaining pair grappled for holds in unmentionable parts of his anatomy. With agonised squeals, locked in each other's embrace, they would crash backwards into the bouncing neoprene. There was usually a round of applause from the onlookers.

Another activity that was sure to draw a crowd was the task of getting Fletcher up a ladder. We are all familiar with the problems presented by these vertical challenges, which look so simple at high water but take on alarming proportions several hours (and probably a few drinks) later. Tough it may be for humankind to make the climb with ease and dignity, but it's far harder for our four-legged friends. Fletcher, of course, had to put his mountaineering skills to the test. We'd gone ashore for a meal leaving him, so we thought, firmly shut in behind closed washboards. It was the work of a moment for him to butt his great head straight through the top board and make a mad leap for the quay, intent on joining in the fun. To give him his due, he did make it about ten feet up the ladder before the force of gravity overtook him. He hurtled backwards towards the deck, bounced painfully off a stanchion, and was catapulted, yelping, into the water. He never forgot, and thereafter had to be transported up ladders clasped lovingly to the Skipper's bosom, casting terrified glances all around, like a toddler recovering from a nightmare.

One further snag to choosing a Dalmatian as a sailing crony is that they are conspicuous dogs. No doubt other large breeds have their off moments too, but their misdeeds don't so often come home to roost as those of our spotty pal. Fletcher soon became notorious around our favourite cruising grounds and we'd find, on entering port, that his fame had spread before us and people were already snatching up their infant children, abandoning any attempts to renew varnish or deck paint, or drawing their dinghies up alongside defensively in the hope we'd go and berth somewhere else.

The charges laid against him ranged through many areas, and honesty compels me to admit there was justification for all of them. He did indeed take a positive delight in fouling fishemen's nets as they were laid out to dry on the quay, preferring to put on this display when the fishermen were actually working in them. And he did pick fights with local dogs in strange ports, often displaying his stunning lack of intelligence by taking on the mangiest, most battle-scarred band of cut-throats he could find, taking a thorough hammering, and then limping home bedaubed with blood and spittle to do his wounded soldier act on the settee cushions. And he had, on more than one occasion, wolfed down the entire breakfast of neighbouring crews who'd been unwise enough to leave it unattended for the few seconds it took to nip below for the marmalade. But he wasn't *all* bad.

He was a pretty effective watchdog, for a start. Nothing has ever been stolen from our boat while Fletcher was around. But then there was that one occasion... We'd been gale-bound, yet again, for quite a time and were getting rather bored with the whole thing. Reasoning that a hook that had held for two wild days would hold for one more evening we decided to take a break from nail-biting and reward ourselves with a dinner ashore. Scarcely had we dipped our spoons into the prawn cocktails when the wind and tide arose together and we dashed to the restaurant window to watch, with sinking hearts, our boat take off on a dramatic drag across the bay.

Already fearing that we would be too late, we dashed to our dinghy but were relieved to see, as we thrashed our way through the spray, that willing hands from nearby craft had tackled the problem and were clambering aboard to get the engine started and avert disaster. But we'd reckoned without

Fletcher. Letting forth a volley of deafening barks and fearsome growls, he refused to allow them anywhere near the controls. Fortunately for us, just one soul was brave enough to apply the 'well-placed boot' theory of dog psychology and the engine fired in the nick of time. And when we'd bandaged him up and filled him full of whisky, he was really quite forgiving about the whole thing too.

Perhaps the most bizarre encounter occurred one year in the west of Ireland when we'd once again left Fletcher 'safely' shut into the saloon while we took the air ashore. Strolling back after an hour or so's absence we were surprised to see a large gaggle of people clustered together at the very end of the pier while the remaining length was deserted, apart from a large black and white shape cavorting around, barking lustily. Pausing only for the skipper and I to exchange I-told-you-so style glares and for the kids to break into howls of delight, we cantered to the rescue. Immediately we were harangued on all sides by fellow yachtsmen, fishermen and tourists all speaking, for unfathomable reasons, a mixture of slow, shouted English and tortured schoolboy-French. It took quite a while to discover that the cause of the panic was the name of our home port, painted in bold letters on our stern. While 'Quoile' is well known in our own locality, as a river and the title of the yacht club that stands at its extremity, to those not familiar with it the name had a disturbingly foreign ring. It had been decided by a few, and spread by mass hysteria to the many, that we were a continental boat in disguise and that therefore Fletcher was a wild, rabid, continental dog, being smuggled in under wraps. It took a lot of fast talking and a great deal of soothing of wounded feelings on all sides to prevent the police being called and persuade everyone to calm down. Even so, there was a fair amount of animosity left hanging in the atmosphere. We didn't stay long in port.

It was a sad irony that, at the end of an eight-year reign of sailing terror and misdeeds, Fletcher was to pass on to a better place via the wheels of a speeding car, rather than being keel-

hauled by an irate yachtsman. We and (surprisingly enough) many of our friends felt the loss keenly, although I can't doubt that there were some who allowed themselves a small sigh of relief too. If they did, it was short-lived, for we weren't long in getting a replacement pup, also spotty, who is fast proving every bit as much a trial as his illustrious forefather.

In fact Beaufort (named for his ability to produce winds of varying strength and varying acceptability) has already gone one better than his predecessor by opening his account on someone else's boat, rather than our own.

'Do bring him with you', enthused our friends when issuing our invitation. 'We've never had a dog on board before.'

The boat was a magnificent fifty-footer, lovingly cared for and immaculate throughout, with lush, deep-buttoned upholstery and high-gloss parquet flooring from stem to stern. It didn't begin too well when Beaufort insisted on taking the skipper's own personal bunk as the only one to suit his aristocratic needs, and things got worse when he then proceeded to live up to his name by producing terrifying pongs at regular intervals during the skipper's offwatch snooze. As the fifth dank cloud wafted into the skipper's nostrils and made his eyes water, he reacted in a remarkably understanding manner.

"OK, Beaufort," he said resignedly. "We'll make a deal. You do it in my face, and I'll do it in yours . . . just as long as everyone knows," he added, turning a weary eye on the rest of us, "that this is a *team* effort!"

That might have been the end of our troubles but, alas, we soon ran into a strong headwind and in the ensuing hard beat there was no rest for anyone, least of all Beaufort. Unable to find a peaceful and secure spot anywhere, he was thrown about wildly for hours on end. Each time the yacht slammed over onto a different tack, those of us up in the cockpit were treated to the sight of a leggy black and white bundle hurtling across the saloon, paws scrabbling frantically for a foothold of any kind. He may have been frightened but he wasn't being hurt so it struck the entire crew as highly amusing at the time. When we at last reached port and went below for a restorative glass of something warming, however, our smiles died on our faces. The settee berths and cushions all looked as though a sudden fall of snow had occurred, so thick was the mantle of white fur, most of it hopelessly embedded in the wildly expensive fabric. But worse still was the floor, once so highly polished and a delight to the eye, that now had the appearance of having been the venue for an amateur ploughing competition.

It took an immense effort of will for the owner's wife to summon up her best social manner to meet the occasion. 'Oh, *please* don't worry about it," she gulped, struggling for breath. "I'm sure he didn't mean to . . . I mean, I think . . . I *hope* it will all polish out all right . . ."

Her husband, and who can blame him, was more forthright. "We've never had a dog on board before," he said heavily, the muscles in his jawline twitching ominously, "And, by God, we never will again!"

I have a notion he won't be rushing to issue a repeat request for *our* company, either.

8

When the deep purple falls

The brain can play funny tricks on you when you're tired. I remember once doing a night watch on a return trip from France; with the wind light and the boat slipping along effortlessly, it was easy to relax into a dreamy frame of mind. The loneliness of the long-distance watchkeeper was no problem either because another boat was keeping steady pace with us, round about where the horizon would have been if I'd been able to see it. Ghosting along under a full spinnaker she made a fine sight and it was cheering to know we were not totally alone out there.

As my trick neared its end I heard the gobbling snorts that usually indicate the Skipper rousing himself for his tour of duty and shortly a steaming mug of something was proffered from the hatchway, closely followed by the man himself. "Feel ready for some company?" he asked, his winning smile somewhat marred by a cocoa moustache. "It's OK, I've got some," I said, nodding towards the ballooning sail glowing silver-white in the distance. "She's been shadowing us for hours. I tried a couple of radio calls but she's not answering. Probably too busy."

The Skipper took a look and then eyed our own hard-sheeted genoa with some incredulity. "If she's flying a spinnaker while we're close-hauled they'll be more than busy," he said, and snatched up the binoculars for a more detailed inspection. "Yes, well," he announced after a moment's thought, "If you'd got a reply on the VHF it would have come via NASA. That's the moon, you b— idiot!"

It took quite a while for his faith in my powers of observation to be restored but really he was in no position to be too critical. On one of our earliest night passages I'd done my sums, got a good fix, given him a clear course to steer and retired below, to be roused from my slumbers by an angrily prodding finger and an urgent whisper. "I don't know what the hell your navigational plans were," he hissed furiously, "But you'd better get up here and do a re-think fast!"

"Whasserr matter?" I muttered, sleepily struggling erect, "We've got nothing to worry us for miles yet . . ." He shoved me roughly up the steps and out into the chilly night air. "Is that a fact?" he said grimly, "In that case, how do you explain this small town we're about to crash into?" And sure enough, dead ahead of us was a wide expanse of twinkling lights with what seemed to be a block of flats at the centre. This time I was the one to remember the binoculars and turn on the mockery, for the 'town' turned out to be an oil-rig under tow from a fleet of tugs. "Oh all right, titter if you must," said the Skipper somewhat sheepishly. "At least it proves I was on the alert . . ."

Certainly, maintaining full concentration can be a problem in the small hours. Even simply staying awake can be hard enough, although usually I don't have too much trouble. By the time I'm dressed for the part, with first the long-johns, then several layers of woolly outers plus a set of stiff oilies with hood pulled up and firmly lashed down over my bobble hat, then a well-tightened harness to anchor the whole lot in place, I find I move with all the fluid grace of a Frankenstein creation. Once I'm wedged in behind the ship's wheel, arms and legs extended like a patient in traction, getting sufficiently relaxed to nod off is a virtual impossibility.

The Skipper, on the other hand, is one of those folk who would snore through Armageddon, and keeping him on his toes requires drastic measures. When he feels sleep stealing over him, he employs a novel technique. Having worked out that it takes approximately ten minutes from a light first appearing on the horizon to the last moment when avoiding action is possible, he takes a stance in the companionway where he can absorb a modicum of heat from the saloon and support his elbows on either side of the hatch. The clever bit is that in this position it takes exactly ten minutes for him to drift into dreamland, and when he does his elbows lose their grip, his body slithers floorward and his chin slams into the hatch cover with a resounding thud that jolts him, and usually me, awake. It doesn't do much for my rest but it is at least a constant reminder that he's still with us.

And that's something that used to worry me a lot during our early night passages together. Unlike me, he doesn't establish himself in a relatively comfy spot and stay put. He likes to be busy, and if he's not checking the dinghy lashings or changing the jib he'll be wandering about the foredeck in head phones playing with the RDF, just for practice. Although he's on a solemn oath not to do this without being firmly clipped on, it can still be trifle disconcerting to glance up from your sleeping bag and see only an empty cockpit and auto-piloted wheel jerking erratically in the gloom. I'm not too sure of the value of the harness anyway. As a pal once pointed out to me, if the boat's on self-steering and everyone else is dead to the world below decks, the unlucky chap who pitches over the side at the start of his watch isn't going to be in grand shape when he's pulled out later, having been towed at six knots for several hours. So my sleep is interrupted by frequent trips to the hatch just to make sure there is still a burly shape hunched somewhere about the decks.

Not that I would get much real sleep anyway. It's not just my natural nervousness that's at fault. Unless the sea is mirror-smooth, and that's a rarity to be prized, I find it incredibly difficult to tune out my surroundings and let sleep take over. For one thing, I haven't yet found a truly non-slip sleeping bag, so if the boat is pitching I alternate between being thrust out of

87

its enveloping warmth like a reluctant moth emerging from its cocoon, or vanishing into its fusty depths and wakening in a sweaty and claustrophobic prison. If the boat is rolling, I spend my time either flattening my nose against unyielding locker doors or swinging precariously in the lee-cloth like Drake in his hammock until either the knots or the fabric give way and dump me unceremoniously on the floor. If it's really rough I find I get most peace by making a nest of settee cushions on the floor itself and bedding down there, but even this isn't entirely successful. The motion may be easier but the sound of water sloshing about in the tanks just a few inches from my ear gives me bad dreams; and every time the Skipper comes down to brew himself a quick cuppa he gets his wellies entangled with my outstretched feet and collapses on top of me with a startled cry.

I imagine that heavy racing crews have similar problems of space allocation but at least they don't have the traumas, so familiar to us family cruisers, of getting the children happily installed for the night. Some youngsters treat the whole thing as a wonderful adventure, but ours are not of this stoical variety and don't take kindly to being lashed into a bed that's leaping around like an unbroken colt and being told to shut up and go to sleep because Mum and Dad are busy. I've tried everything from favourite teddy bears to Mickey Mouse nightlights, but it seems that only devoted parental attention will do the trick. It's a real challenge to squat uncomfortably on the square foot of floor space in the forepeak with the boat dancing like a dervish and read a bedtime story while clutching a flickering flashlight. As the lines leap about before your eyes and you rush to get to the end of the tale before your stomach gives in to the queasiness that's gradually stealing over you, the child will rear up in the bed, glaring at you with indignation. "You missed the best bit! Now you'll have to start *all* over again!"

Once we made the mistake of allowing our junior child to bring along her most irritating toy, a tinny musical box with a repertoire of the first two lines of the Seven Dwarfs' song and nothing else, in the hope that she could use it to lull herself to sleep. In fact, it poved quite effective but only by continuous playing of the same wretched jingle over and over again until the Skipper and I feared for our sanity. We'd groan as we heard the first cranking of the handle and then away it would tinkle, "Hi ho, hi ho, it's off to work we go . . . tiddle om pom pom, tiddle om pom pom . . ." until it enmeshed itself in our brains and refused to be shaken out. We heard it in the rhythmic thump of the engine, in the splashing of the waves, and it echoed in our heads as we went about our work, precluding all rational thought. "To hell with the *hi ho*," muttered the Skipper one night as we sat at the chart table with our fingers in our ears, "The minute she closes her eyes, I'm giving it the heave-ho. It's either it, or me . . ." I managed to dissuade him on the grounds of extreme cruelty to innocent babes, but later on that night I caught him with a screwdriver in his hand and an evil leer on his face; and next day the infernal contraption had developed a mysterious fault that resisted all attempts at repair.

Since reaching his teenage years, our senior offspring has shown a desire to join in our night watchkeeping routines, which is something of a help. He lacks the experience to take a turn alone but it does mean one can take one's time over chartwork or nip below for a brew-up with reasonable confidence that he'll mention it if we're about to ram anything large amidships. Or does it? There was that occasion when we were cruising with another boat and I left him in charge while I paid an overdue visit to the heads. It took rather longer than anticipated, what with the layers of restrictive clothing and all.

"All clear?" I asked cheerfully, as I returned to my post. "Affirmative," responded the lad, who watches rather too much TV. "Can't see the others though. They must have changed course . . ." But a quick survey revealed that, far from being miles away, they were in fact hidden behind our billowing genoa and we were about to enter their cockpit by plunging our bows through their transom.

But he's pleasant company anyway, especially since we happen to share the same taste in music. The Skipper, being a shanty-man by nature, doesn't have our enthusiasm for hard rock and complains bitterly of we impose it in him. So to enliven the watching hours, the lad and I sling our personal stereos under the oilies and clap on the 'phones so we can enjoy a little up-beat entertainment without enraging him. Unfortunately we are inclined to get a trifle carried away by the driving rhythms and start singing along, with drumming accompaniment on the coachroof. As we're each tuned in to different tapes the Skipper, desperately trying to grab forty winks in his bunk, receives jarring amateur versions of our individual selections from Queen's Greatest Hits, in stereo and at full blast. We usually wind up being ordered to our beds in disgrace, but only I get the "At your age, you ought to know better" line.

Mind you, he's normally very understanding about being roused from his sleep, which is just as well because I'm known for taking his "Wake me up if you have any doubts about anything" instruction rather more literally than he would wish. I've dragged him on deck to give his opinion on tankers on collision courses that turned out to be five miles off, unexplained quick-flashing buoys that were actually car headlights passing lines of coastal trees, and once I even hauled him out to share my delight in a shoal of gleaming silver fish that were keeping pace with us only to have it icily pointed out that I was watching the reflections of our masthead lights in the wavelets.

To give him due credit he has never refused one of these calls to arms, working on the sound principle that a dozen false alarms are better than one potential emergency ignored; but I suffer for it later, when he gets together with his fellow skippers to swop 'idiot crew' stories. And he's good enough to resist the temptation to turn the tables on me too, probably because he reckons it's easier to handle any situation singlehandedly than to invite me up to stumble about sleepily

. . . about to enter their cockpit.

and generally get under foot. If he should run across a fleet of drift fishermen intent on a confrontation, the first I know about it is the crashing of a flailing boom and strings of muffled curses. Since my slumbers are in any case filled with visions of juddering encounters with unseen baulks of timber or pods of snoozing whales, I clutch at the sleeping bag and wait for a sudden inrush of water before dismissing it all as yet another bad dream.

Some of our land-based friends have odd ideas about night sailing. One even imagined that we all simply drop anchor and park through the dark hours. "How on earth do you find your way?" asked another, clearly seeing it as the equivalent of groping round the sitting room, falling over furniture as you hunt for a light switch. In fact navigational marks are far easier to spot when they're lit, although if we're doing quite a bit of buoy-hopping the Skipper and I have been known to have the odd heated debate about the individual characteristics of the twinkles we pick up. It's not easy to keep one eye on the bobbing light and the other on the second hand of your watch as you count out the flashes. If you try to do it as a team it's worse. "When it starts again say 'now' and when it finishes say 'stop'," he instructs, juggling with his Seiko in the faint loom of the binnacle. "Ready? Now!" "I thought that was supposed to be my line?" I respond, bobbing and weaving like a prize-fighter as the sail flaps in and out of my line of vision. "Right, it's starting again NOW . . . er, no it isn't . . . yes . . . no . . . hang on a minute, I've lost it again . . ."

After a few minutes of this we usually give it up as a bad job and resort to the more traditional methods of approximating seconds, and with two hooded figures standing there with eyes fixed on the far horizon while they chant "One elephant, two elephant . . ." you'd think some obscure religious ritual was being enacted. If we happen to get elephants of different sizes it merely comes out as a confusing burble, like a crowd scene from a schoolboys' *Julius Caesar*.

But in spite of the traumas I must confess that I do enjoy a night passage. For one thing, it's never dark for very long and if there's no cloud cover the contrast between the deep velvet sky and the bright stabs of starlight is a delight to the eye. I like to claim the watches at each end of the night so each quarter hour is marked by subtle transformations in my surroundings. Otherwise the time can hang heavy on my hands, and I have to resort to little tricks and treats to see me through. I gather around me a variety of goodies and ration myself strictly to a toffee every fifteen minutes, a mouthful of nuts every thirty, and a sandwich and brew-up to go with my hourly log entries. In between I pass the time with the odd illicit cigarette or two, a bad habit and one which the Skipper firmly frowns on below decks. Smoking on watch is really more a gesture of defiance than a pleasure, though; it takes five minutes of steady cursing and half a box of matches to get the thing lit at all, my fingers freeze, and even on a still night the wind of passage makes it burn down like a fuse making for the powder-keg. I wind up with a half-inch of fiercely glowing butt that adheres to my lips as if super-glued and is sheer agony to prise loose. And when I flick it casually over the side it's ten to one the breeze will chuck it straight back and then there's a panicky scramble to find it before either I or the ship go up in flames.

We work 2½-hour watches at night — two hours are spent alone with one's thoughts and the remaining half is meant to be passed in relaxed chat while we share a cuppa, update each other on our progress, and discuss life, the universe and everything. In fact, conversation tends to be a bit desultory in the changeover period, with the waking partner still stiff and

"One elephant, two elephant . . ."

93

furry-tongued from sleep and the retiring one — knowing that rest and relief are a wink away – suddenly sliding into oblivion in mid-sentence. If it happens to be lashing rain and a strong blow, our pally handovers take on a much more abrupt tone and exchanges are limited to "Right, you're on. Course in the log." as we pass each other on the companionway steps.

One of my most joyful sailing memories is of a night passage from Brittany to the Scillies, made in perfect weather with calm seas and just enough gentle breeze to keep up a leisurely pace under sail. From the start, we knew it was going to be one of those special experiences, for just as we were ending a relaxed evening meal with some excellent French coffee and small cognac to warm the blood we heard the unmistakable sound of a whale's spout just off our bows. A trio of large rorquals were cruising towards us with a purposeful air. The Skipper drew in a jittery breath as they dived with a gentle sigh and a majestic upward flick of their great tails to pass beneath our keel. "Don't worry, they've gone down," I said soothingly. "I can see that," he muttered crossly, "I'm more concerned about where they're going to come up!" But they surfaced at a safe distance on the other side of us and, giving us one more deep-throated blow of farewell, moved on their way.

We felt we'd been given a rare privilege; and we watched the sun slipping down into a rippling, honey-coloured sea, feeling a warm inner glow that was not entirely due to the cognac. Soon bright stars began to pinpoint the deepening sky; with no moon it would have been a dark night had not the summer phosphorescence been at its peak. With the cool of night the wind freshened slightly and as our speed increased the hissing wake spread out astern in a million tumbling sparkles, while each dip of the bows threw up a luminous foam that bathed the jib in an unearthly green light. Our watch system was abandoned as neither of us wanted to retire and miss a moment of this spectacular display, but at last the effect began to fade and the Skipper insisted that one us should get some rest in preparation for the day ahead.

Reluctantly I agreed to turn in but I had barely settled myself ready to doze off when there was an urgent whisper from the cockpit. "Hey, get up here quick! We've got company!" I was half-expecting a warning blast from a speeding oil tanker as I struggled into my clothes, but instead the saloon was suddenly

PEYTON

filled with a vibrant chorus of chirrups and clicks as if an aviary of budgerigars had been let loose below. I hurried on deck to find the Skipper grinning with delight as a school of perhaps fifty dolphins frolicked around our hull. They were diving under the boat and emerging with joyous leaps on the other side. Some were bounding along in our wake and a couple were playing with our trailing log, tossing the spinner out of the water as if it were a toy. At the bows a gang was speeding along close to the boat, taking turns to nudge in front and enjoy a helter-skelter ride on the pressure-wave at the stem. The sky was already brightening to a clear dawn and I could see the small, glittering eyes and apparently smiling mouths of the leaders, so close that I could almost lean down and touch their dorsal fins. They stayed with us for about half an hour while we crowed with pleasure and exhausted all the film in our cameras, and then they were gone as silently and unexpectedly as they'd arrived, as if by some conjuror's trick. Certainly they had been magical to us.

Later on that day the wind piped up to give us a wearisome plunge into a head sea, we made a mistake in navigation that gave us a lengthy and quite unnecessary detour to find port, we put an expensive rip in the jib and ran out of gas so we could eat only cold food. Normally I would have been depressed and irritable and asking myself that perennial question: why on earth do I go sailing at all? I didn't, though. This time, at least — I knew.